LEISURE ARTS' BEST

TeddyBear
·TREASURY·

LEISURE ARTS, INC.
and
OXMOOR HOUSE, INC.

TeddyBear
·T R E A S U R Y·

Teddy bears are a symbol of the innocence of childhood, the comfort of family and friends, and our own capacity to love. With their wholesome charm, it's easy to see why our furry little friends have been cherished ever since the early 1900's, when they were named after President Theodore "Teddy" Roosevelt. Our must-have Treasury of Teddy Bears contains an abundance of irresistible scenes that remind us of our childhood buddy's talent for sharing a belly laugh or offering a snuggly bear hug. This versatile collection includes sweatshirts and samplers, afghans and aprons, towels and totes, and more, in a volume brimming over with ideas for home decorating, clothing, and gifts. Like peanut butter and jelly, teddy bears and cross stitch are such perfect partners that you'll "bearly" be able to put down this book!

EDITORIAL STAFF
Vice President and Editor-in-Chief:
Anne Van Wagner Childs
Executive Director: Sandra Graham Case
Editorial Director: Susan Frantz Wiles
Publications Director: Carla Bentley
Creative Art Director: Gloria Bearden
Senior Graphics Art Director: Melinda Stout

EDITORIAL
Managing Editor: Linda L. Trimble
Associate Editors: Darla Burdette Kelsay and
Janice Teipen Wojcik
Assistant Editors: Tammi Williamson Bradley,
Terri Leming Davidson, and Karen Walker
Copy Editor: Laura Lee Weland

TECHNICAL
Senior Publications Editor: Sherry Taylor O'Connor
Special Projects Editor: Connie White Irby
Senior Production Assistant: Martha H. Carle

ART
Book/Magazine Graphics Art Director:
Diane M. Hugo
Senior Production Graphics Illustrator: Guniz Jernigan
Production Graphics Illustrator: Bridgett Shrum

BUSINESS STAFF
Publisher: Bruce Akin
Vice President, Marketing: Guy A. Crossley
Vice President and General Manager: Thomas L. Carlisle
Retail Sales Director: Richard Tignor
Vice President, Retail Marketing: Pam Stebbins
Retail Marketing Director: Margaret Sweetin
Retail Customer Services Manager: Carolyn Pruss
General Merchandise Manager: Russ Barnett
Vice President, Finance: Tom Siebenmorgen
Distribution Director: Ed M. Strackbein

Library of Congress Catalog Number 97-73652
Hardcover ISBN 0-8487-4165-X
Softcover ISBN 1-57486-077-1

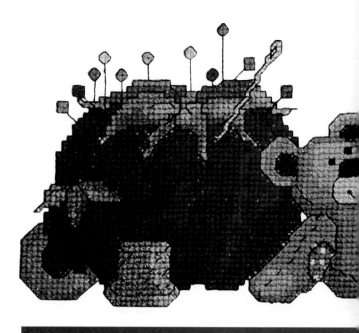

Table of Contents

Teddy Bear Reunion

When relatives or longtime friends gather for a visit, their reunion is bound to rekindle fond memories and inspire lots of love and laughter. The heartwarming scenes in this collection recall such tender moments. With open arms and friendly smiles, the extended teddy bear family in our Bear Family Welcome will lend a touch of warmth and hospitality to your home and remind you of your own beloved kinfolk.

"...amily and Me Welcome Jhee"

"My Family and I"

X	DMC	1/4X	B'ST	ANC.	COLOR	X	DMC	1/4X	1/2X	ANC.	COLOR	X	DMC	1/4X	B'ST	ANC.	COLOR
•	blanc			2	white	■	434			310	dk brown	▨	729			890	gold
-	ecru			387	ecru	▦	435			1046	brown	+	738			361	dk beige
⊞	310		/	403	black	✦	436			1045	lt brown	▦	739			387	beige
■	311		/	148	dk navy	⊠	437			362	vy lt brown	○	760			1022	lt rose
△	312			979	navy	▲	453	/		231	beige grey	◆	761			1021	pink
◇	320			215	green	■	498			1005	red	⊕	762			234	pearl grey
T	322			978	lt navy	✳	543			933	vy lt tan	▧	801	/	/*	359	dk golden brown
★	333			119	dk purple	▼	645			273	vy dk grey	□	839			360	vy dk beige brown
+	340			118	purple	□	646			8581	dk grey	✕	840			379	dk beige brown
○	341			117	lavender	▒	647	/	▒	1040	grey	▼	841			378	beige brown
▽	347			1025	lt red	□	648			900	lt grey	▽	842			388	lt beige brown
★	367	/		217	dk green	-	676			891	lt gold	◒	844			1041	charcoal
⊕	368			214	lt green	○	677			886	vy lt gold	+	927			848	blue green
=	369			1043	vy lt green	▲	680			901	dk gold	-	928			274	lt blue green
✕	422			373	tan	✰	725	/		305	yellow	✦	930			1035	dk blue
◎	433			358	vy dk brown	⊕	726			295	lt yellow	◆	931			1034	blue

"Ne Welcome Jhee"

X	DMC	¼X	ANC.	COLOR
×	932		1033	lt blue
⊡	3072	◩	847	vy lt grey
☆	3328		1024	rose
⊕	3713		1020	lt pink
▽	3747		120	lt lavender
+	3752	☐	1032	vy lt blue
=	3821			dk yellow
○	3828			dk tan
•	310			black French Knot
☐				Blue area indicates last row of left section of design.
*				Use 2 strands of floss.

The design was stitched over 2 fabric threads on a 22" x 14" piece of Antique White Lugana (25 ct). Three strands of floss were used for Cross Stitch, 1 strand for Backstitch and Half Cross Stitch, and 2 strands for French Knots, unless otherwise noted in the color key. It was custom framed.

Design by Darcy Gerdes.
Needlework adaptation by Jane Chandler.

CHATTER HAT
BEARS

*Donning their
Sunday bonnets,
this trio of
beribboned bears
gathers to pass an
afternoon chatting
about the latest
fashion trends.*

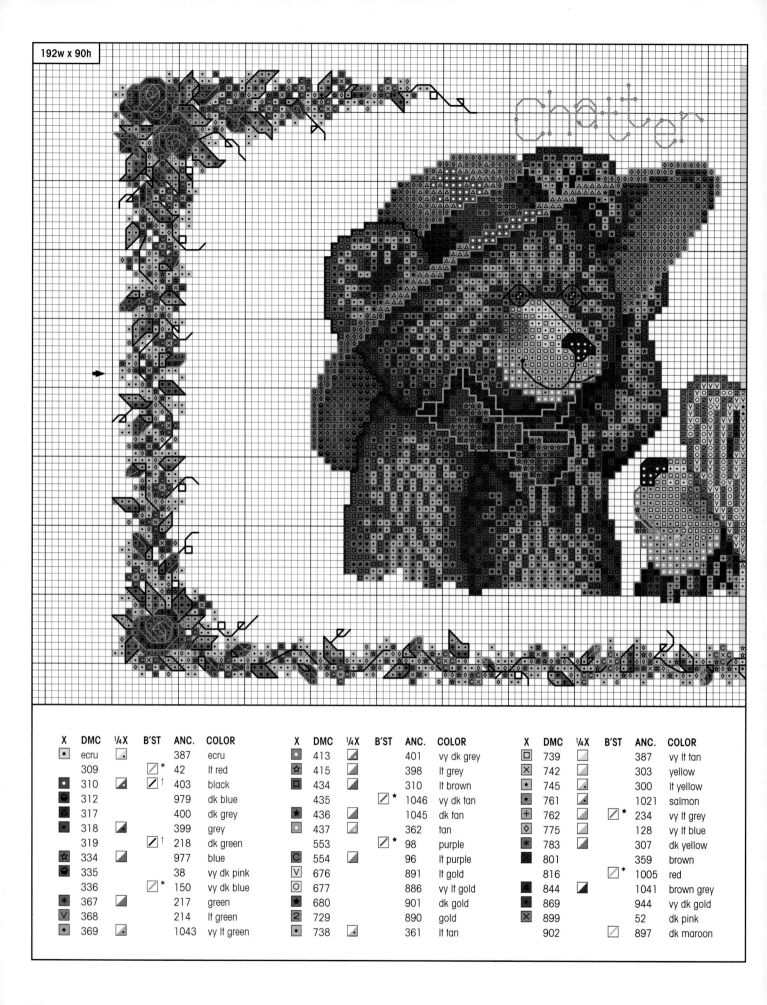

192w x 90h

X	DMC	¼X	B'ST	ANC.	COLOR
•	ecru			387	ecru
	309		/*	42	lt red
•	310		/†	403	black
	312			979	dk blue
▲	317			400	dk grey
★	318			399	grey
	319		/†	218	dk green
☆	334			977	blue
●	335			38	vy dk pink
	336		/*	150	vy dk blue
✳	367			217	green
V	368			214	lt green
•	369			1043	vy lt green

X	DMC	¼X	B'ST	ANC.	COLOR
•	413			401	vy dk grey
☆	415			398	lt grey
▣	434			310	lt brown
	435		/*	1046	vy dk tan
★	436			1045	dk tan
◉	437			362	tan
	553		/*	98	purple
C	554			96	lt purple
V	676			891	lt gold
O	677			886	vy lt gold
■	680			901	dk gold
2	729			890	gold
•	738			361	lt tan

X	DMC	¼X	B'ST	ANC.	COLOR
□	739			387	vy lt tan
✕	742			303	yellow
•	745			300	lt yellow
•	761			1021	salmon
+	762		/*	234	vy lt grey
◇	775			128	vy lt blue
✳	783			307	dk yellow
■	801			359	brown
	816		/*	1005	red
▲	844			1041	brown grey
✳	869			944	vy dk gold
✕	899			52	dk pink
	902		/	897	dk maroon

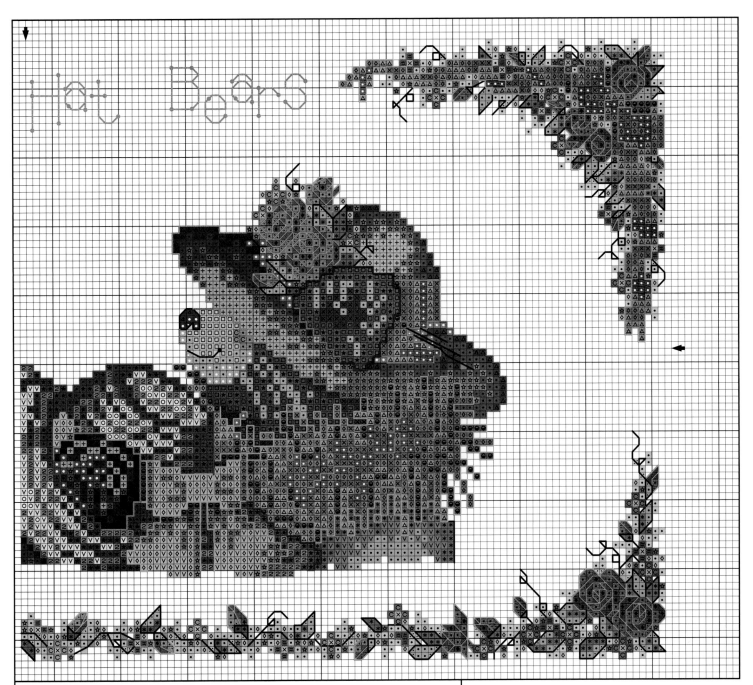

X	DMC	1/4X	B'ST	ANC.	COLOR
◉	915	◪	◆	1029	dk mauve
▦	917	◪		89	mauve
	938		◪	381	dk brown
◇	962			75	pink
◉	963			73	vy lt pink
V	3325			129	lt blue
☆	3607	◪		87	lt mauve
△	3685			1028	maroon
◆	3712	◪		1023	dk salmon
C	3713			1020	lt salmon
△	3716			25	lt pink
	3799		◪ ◆	236	steel grey
●	310				black French Knot

X	DMC	
◉	902	dk maroon French Knot
◉	915	dk mauve French Knot
▢		Blue area indicates first row of right section of design.

* Use vy dk blue for center hat ribbon, red for roses, and lt red for all other.

† Use black for facial features and dk green for all other.

★ Use purple for flowers, vy lt grey for highlights in eyes, and vy dk tan for all other.

◆ Use dk mauve for letters and flowers and steel grey for all other.

The design was stitched over 2 fabric threads on a 24" x 16" piece of Cream Lugana (25 ct). Three strands of floss were used for Cross Stitch, 2 strands for Backstitch and French Knots in letters, and 1 strand for all other Backstitch and French Knots. It was custom framed.

Design by Darcy Gerdes.
Needlework adaptation by Jane Chandler.

TEDDY BEAR REUNION

Assembled for a family portrait, these country cousins will steal your heart! The cuddly clan offers a charming border for our afghan, which is sure to delight a "beary" special someone.

1. 31w x 28h

2. 180w x 35h

X	DMC	1/4X	B'ST	ANC.	COLOR	X	DMC	1/4X	B'ST	ANC.	COLOR
•	blanc	✓		2	white	−	739	✓		387	cream
◖	310	✓	✓	403	black	•	822	✓		390	lt beige
■	347		✓	1025	red	■	838			380	vy dk brown
✳	433	✓		358	vy dk tan	✶	839	✓		360	dk brown
◖	434	✓		310	dk tan	◼	840	✓		379	brown
V	435	✓		1046	tan	+	841	✓		378	lt brown
•	436	✓		1045	lt tan	−	930	✓	✓	1035	blue
✳	610			889	vy dk khaki	◇	932	✓	✓	1033	lt blue
◖	611	✓		898	dk khaki	☆	3072			847	vy lt grey
+	612	✓		832	khaki	✕	3712	✓	✓	1023	lt red
4	613			831	lt khaki	◼	3790	✓		393	vy dk beige
◖	642	✓		392	dk beige	●	310				black French Knot
2	644			830	beige	◼	Grey area indicates first row of bottom section				
◉	646			8581	dk grey		of design.				
+	647	✓		1040	grey	◻	Blue lines indicate raised border of				
•	648	✓		900	lt grey		stitching area.				
☆	738	✓		361	vy lt tan						

The designs were stitched over 2 fabric threads on a 45" x 58" piece (standard afghan size) of Ivory Abby Cloth (18 ct).

Referring to Diagram for placement of designs on afghan, center and stitch **Design #1** in corner stitching areas. Center **Design #2** in stitching area of each short end (**Design #2** fits exactly in stitching area of short end). Six strands of floss were used for Cross Stitch, 2 strands for black Backstitch and French Knots, and 3 strands for all other Backstitch.

For afghan, cut selvages from fabric; measure 5½" from raw edge of fabric and pull out one fabric thread. Fringe fabric up to missing thread. Repeat for each side. Tie an overhand knot at each corner with 4 horizontal and 4 vertical fabric threads. Working from corners, use 8 fabric threads for each knot until all threads are knotted.

Designs by Jane Chandler.

Some of our fondest childhood memories are of the fun times spent hanging out with our best friends. Whether you stitch this cute design to resemble a snapshot or use only a portion of it on a cozy afghan, these true-blue bear buddies will remind you of your own playful pals.

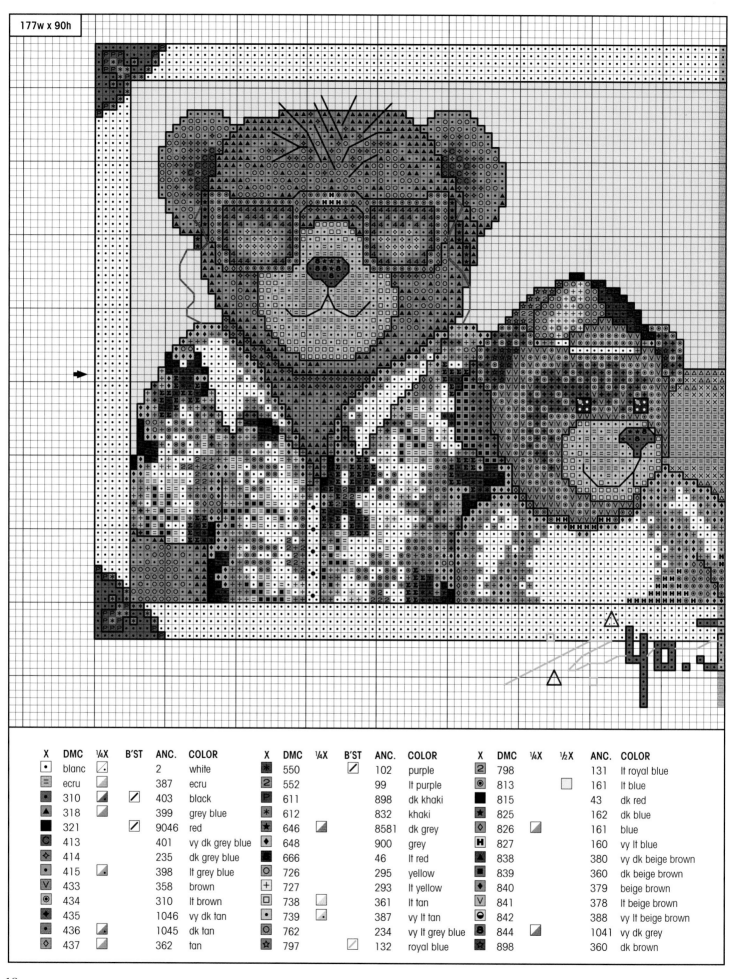

X	DMC	¼X	B'ST	ANC.	COLOR	X	DMC	¼X	B'ST	ANC.	COLOR	X	DMC	¼X	½X	ANC.	COLOR
•	blanc			2	white	✹	550			102	purple	2	798			131	lt royal blue
=	ecru			387	ecru	2	552			99	lt purple	⊙	813			161	lt blue
⬤	310			403	black	P	611			898	dk khaki	■	815			43	dk red
▲	318			399	grey blue	✳	612			832	khaki	★	825			162	dk blue
■	321			9046	red	★	646			8581	dk grey	◇	826			161	blue
C	413			401	vy dk grey blue	◆	648			900	grey	H	827			160	vy lt blue
❖	414			235	dk grey blue	■	666			46	lt red	▲	838			380	vy dk beige brown
•	415			398	lt grey blue	O	726			295	yellow	■	839			360	dk beige brown
V	433			358	brown	+	727			293	lt yellow	◆	840			379	beige brown
⊙	434			310	lt brown	▢	738			361	lt tan	V	841			378	lt beige brown
✦	435			1046	vy dk tan	•	739			387	vy lt tan	⊙	842			388	vy lt beige brown
✶	436			1045	dk tan	O	762			234	vy lt grey blue	8	844			1041	vy dk grey
◇	437			362	tan	☆	797			132	royal blue	✹	898			360	dk brown

18

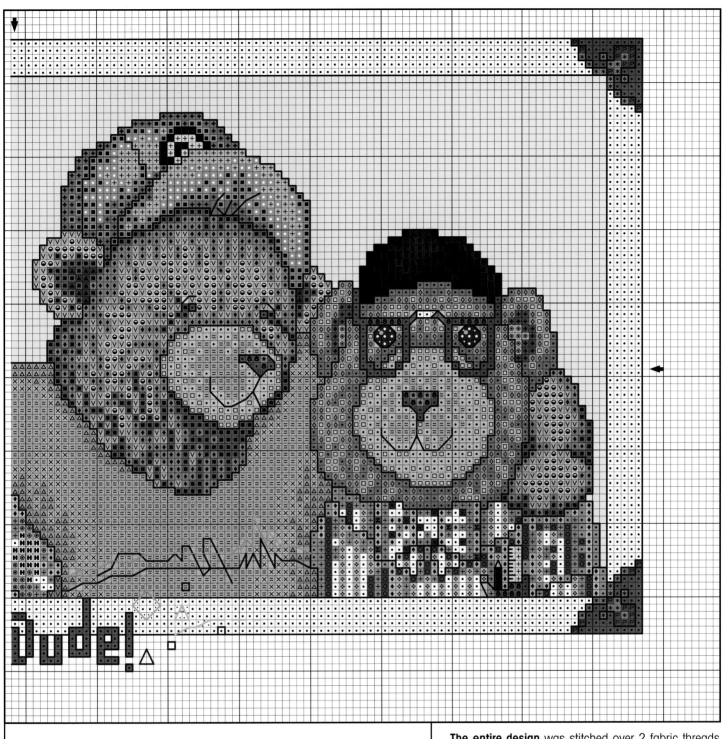

X	DMC	1/4X	B'ST	ANC.	COLOR
■	910	◪		229	dk green
◉	911			205	green
✚	912			209	lt green
■	915	◪ *		1029	dk violet
✦	917			89	violet
▲	924			851	vy dk blue grey
◉	926			850	blue grey
❖	927			848	lt blue grey
●	938	◪		381	vy dk brown
=	954			203	vy lt green
◆	986			246	vy dk green
✕	3033			391	lt beige
✚	3072			847	lt grey

X	DMC	ANC.	COLOR
◩	3607	87	lt violet
•	3768	779	dk blue grey
△	3782	899	beige
○	blanc		white French Knot
●†	310		black French Knot
▧			Pink area indicates first row of right section of design.

* For afghan, use 4 strands. For framed piece, use 3 strands.

† For framed piece, use 2 strands.

The entire design was stitched over 2 fabric threads on a 23" x 16" piece of Cream Lugana (25 ct). Three strands of floss were used for Cross Stitch and 1 strand for Half Cross Stitch, Backstitch, and French Knots, unless otherwise noted in the color key. It was custom framed.

The bears only (refer to photo) were stitched over 2 fabric threads on a 45" x 58" piece (standard afghan size) of Soft White Anne Cloth (18 ct). Six strands of floss were used for Cross Stitch and 2 strands for Backstitch, and French Knots, unless otherwise noted in the color key. For afghan finishing and design placement, see Afghan Finishing, page 143.

Design by Darcy Gerdes.
Needlework adaptation by Jane Chandler.

TEDDY'S TEA PARTY

When little girls throw a tea party, teddy bears are often the guests of honor. Dressed in their finery, these sophisticated friends sip cups of imaginary tea and dream of becoming young ladies. The sweet portrait is sure to delight any little miss.

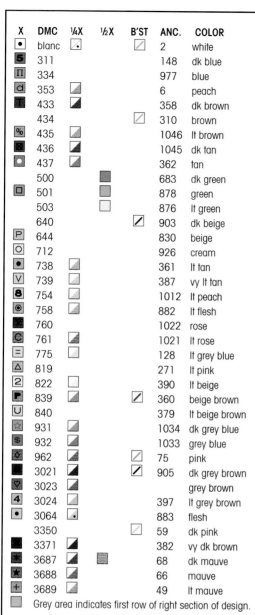

X	DMC	¼X	½X	B'ST	ANC.	COLOR
•	blanc	∴		/	2	white
5	311				148	dk blue
Π	334				977	blue
d	353	/			6	peach
▓	433	/			358	dk brown
	434			/	310	brown
%	435	/			1046	lt brown
▩	436	/			1045	dk tan
○	437	/			362	tan
	500		■		683	dk green
□	501		▨		878	green
	503		□		876	lt green
	640			/	903	dk beige
P	644				830	beige
O	712				926	cream
⊙	738	/			361	lt tan
V	739	/			387	vy lt tan
8	754	/			1012	lt peach
◉	758	/			882	lt flesh
▦	760				1022	rose
C	761	/			1021	lt rose
≡	775	/			128	lt grey blue
△	819				271	lt pink
2	822	□			390	lt beige
▶	839	/		/	360	beige brown
U	840				379	lt beige brown
☆	931	/			1034	dk grey blue
$	932	/			1033	grey blue
◈	962	/		/	75	pink
■	3021	/		/	905	dk grey brown
♡	3023	/				grey brown
4	3024	◪			397	lt grey brown
•	3064	∴			883	flesh
	3350			/	59	dk pink
▓	3371	/			382	vy dk brown
✴	3687	/	▨		68	dk mauve
★	3688	/			66	mauve
+	3689	/			49	lt mauve
▨						Grey area indicates first row of right section of design.

The design was stitched over 2 fabric threads on a 19" x 16" piece of Delicate Teal Jobelan (28 ct). Two strands of floss were used for Cross Stitch and 1 strand for Half Cross Stitch and Backstitch. It was custom framed.

Design by Betty Morris Hamilton.

149w x 112h

STAR-
SPANGLED
BEARS

Nothing brings Americans together like the love we have for our country. Adapted for cross stitch from a watercolor print, this all-American portrait was inspired by the show of patriotism during the Persian Gulf crisis. The flag-waving bears pay tribute to all the men and women who have served our great nation.

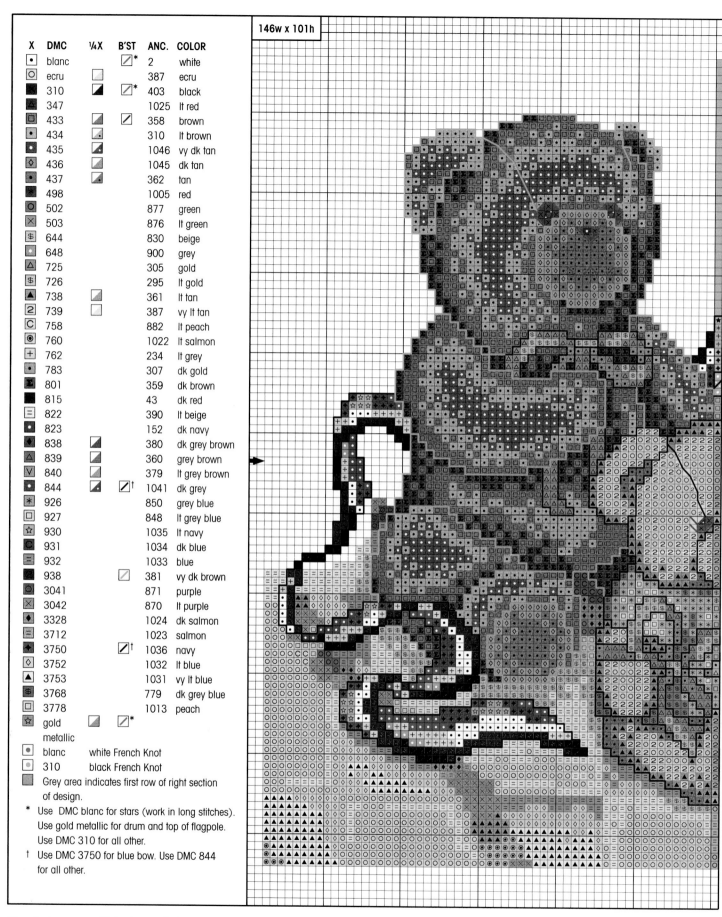

X	DMC	¼X	B'ST	ANC.	COLOR
•	blanc		✓*	2	white
O	ecru	◪		387	ecru
■	310	◪	✓*	403	black
▲	347			1025	lt red
▣	433	◪	✓	358	brown
•	434	◪		310	lt brown
•	435	◪		1046	vy dk tan
◇	436	◪		1045	dk tan
•	437	◪		362	tan
✳	498			1005	red
O	502			877	green
✕	503			876	lt green
$	644			830	beige
▣	648			900	grey
△	725			305	gold
$	726			295	lt gold
▲	738	◪		361	lt tan
2	739	◪		387	vy lt tan
C	758			882	lt peach
◉	760			1022	lt salmon
+	762			234	lt grey
•	783			307	dk gold
▨	801			359	dk brown
■	815			43	dk red
=	822			390	lt beige
▣	823			152	dk navy
◆	838	◪		380	dk grey brown
△	839	◪		360	grey brown
V	840	◪		379	lt grey brown
▣	844	◪	✓†	1041	dk grey
✳	926			850	grey blue
▢	927			848	lt grey blue
☆	930			1035	lt navy
◐	931			1034	dk blue
▤	932			1033	blue
■	938		✓	381	vy dk brown
◎	3041			871	purple
✕	3042			870	lt purple
◆	3328			1024	dk salmon
=	3712			1023	salmon
★	3750		✓†	1036	navy
◇	3752			1032	lt blue
▲	3753			1031	vy lt blue
$	3768			779	dk grey blue
▢	3778			1013	peach
☆	gold metallic	◪	✓*		
•	blanc				white French Knot
●	310				black French Knot

■ Grey area indicates first row of right section of design.

* Use DMC blanc for stars (work in long stitches). Use gold metallic for drum and top of flagpole. Use DMC 310 for all other.

† Use DMC 3750 for blue bow. Use DMC 844 for all other.

146w x 101h

The design was stitched over 2 fabric threads on a 20" x 16" piece of Cream Lugana (25 ct). Three strands of floss were used for Cross Stitch and 1 strand for Backstitch and French Knots. It was custom framed.

Design by Donna Richardson.

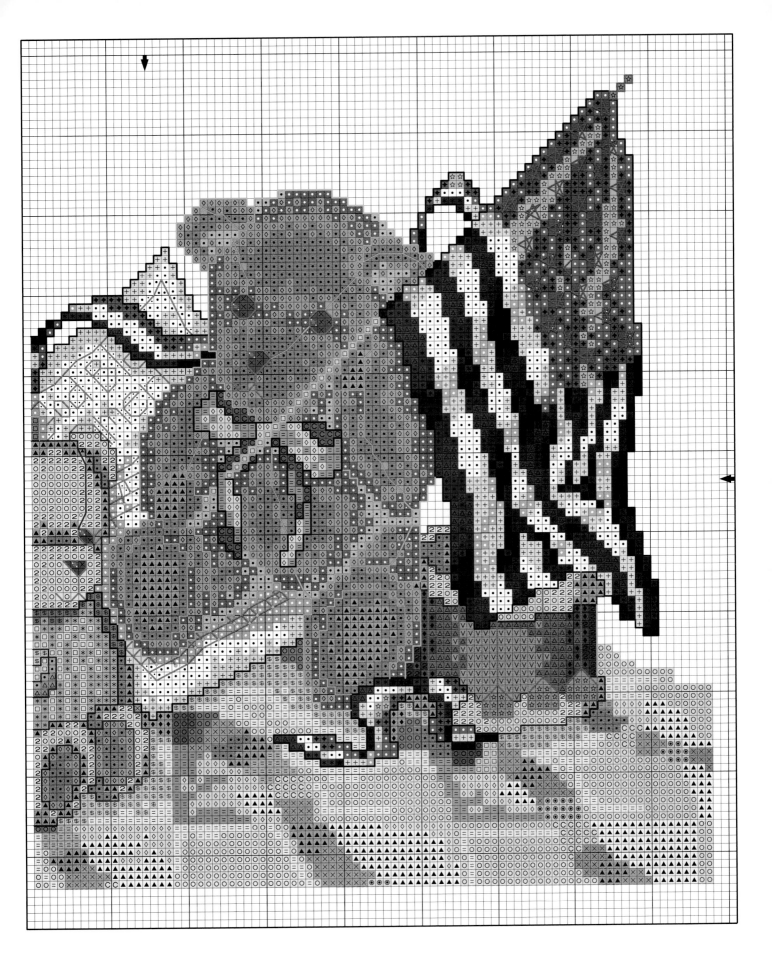

Life's a beach, and the three teddy bear friends in this design are ready to enjoy all it has to offer. Their playful expressions and postures will inspire you to kick up your heels and head for the shore!

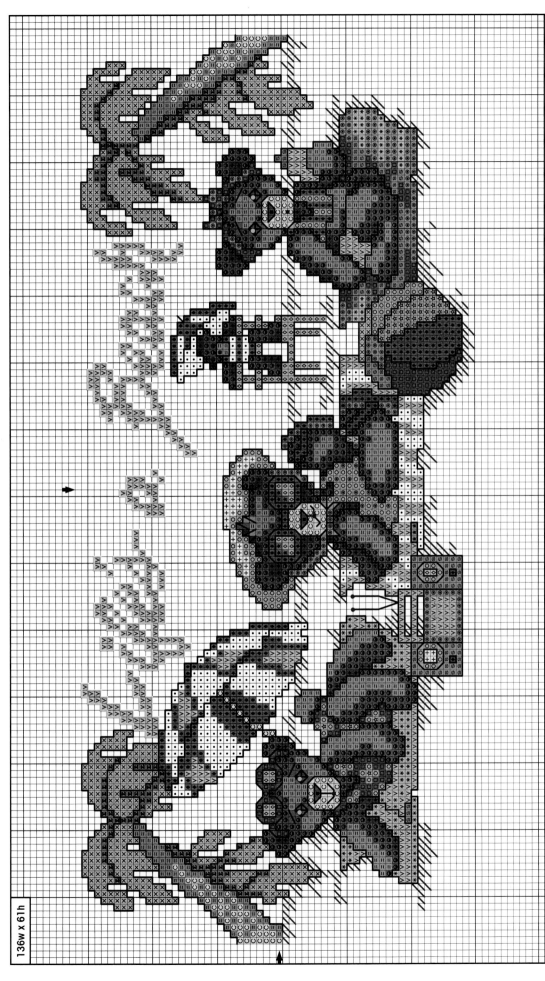

136w x 61h

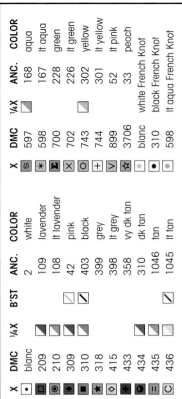

X	1/4X	DMC	ANC.	COLOR
S	◨	597	168	aqua
✳		598	167	lt aqua
▦		700	228	green
✕		702	226	lt green
O		743	302	yellow
+		744	301	lt yellow
V		899	52	lt pink
✪		3706	33	peach
▢		blanc		white French Knot
●		310		black French Knot
▨	◨	598		lt aqua French Knot

X	B'ST	1/4X	DMC	ANC.	COLOR
·			blanc	2	white
▣		◧	209	109	lavender
◉		◧	210	108	lt lavender
▩		◧	309	42	pink
◼	◩	◧	310	403	black
★			318	399	grey
◆			415	398	lt grey
◪		◧	433	358	vy dk tan
◐		◧	434	310	dk tan
‖			435	1046	tan
C	◩	◧	436	1045	lt tan

The entire design was stitched on an 18" x 13" piece of White Aida (14 ct). Two strands of floss were used for Cross Stitch and 1 strand for Backstitch and French Knots. It was custom framed.

Life's a Beach only was stitched on the White Aida (14 ct) insert of a fingertip towel. Two strands of floss were used for Cross Stitch and 1 strand for Backstitch.

Design adapted from a print by Figi Graphics.
Original artwork by Kimberly Stenbo.

THE BEARS' PICNIC

Picnics go hand in hand with summer reunions, and that means visits from curious butterflies and other creatures! The furry family in this design finds time to enjoy a relaxing afternoon in the great outdoors.

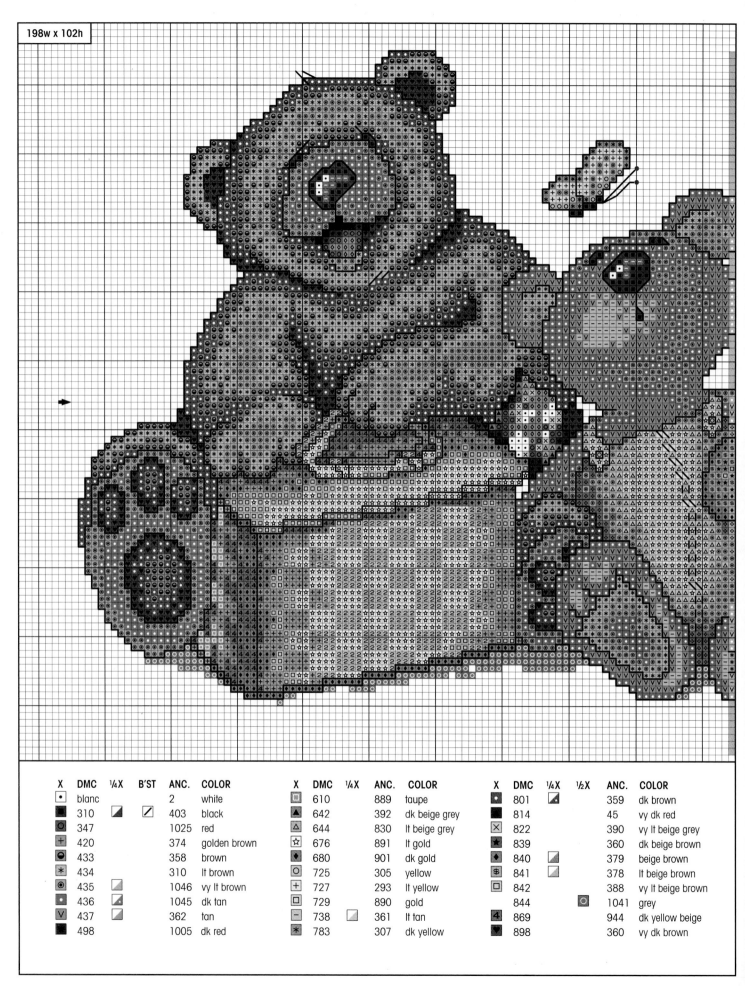

X	DMC	¼X	B'ST	ANC.	COLOR	X	DMC	¼X	ANC.	COLOR	X	DMC	¼X	½X	ANC.	COLOR
•	blanc			2	white	▢	610		889	taupe	●	801	◿		359	dk brown
◼	310	◿	◿	403	black	▲	642		392	dk beige grey	◼	814			45	vy dk red
◔	347			1025	red	△	644		830	lt beige grey	⊠	822			390	vy lt beige grey
+	420			374	golden brown	☆	676		891	lt gold	★	839			360	dk beige brown
◒	433			358	brown	◆	680		901	dk gold	◆	840	◿		379	beige brown
✳	434			310	lt brown	○	725		305	yellow	$	841			378	lt beige brown
◉	435	◿		1046	vy lt brown	+	727		293	lt yellow	▢	842			388	vy lt beige brown
◓	436	◿		1045	dk tan	▢	729		890	gold		844		◎	1041	grey
∨	437	◿		362	tan	–	738	◿	361	lt tan	4	869			944	dk yellow beige
◼	498			1005	dk red	✳	783		307	dk yellow	♥	898			360	vy dk brown

X	DMC	¼X	ANC.	COLOR
⊙	930		1035	dk blue
△	931		1034	blue
☆	932		1033	lt blue
2	3045		888	yellow beige
◇	3328		1024	lt red
❋	3750		1036	vy dk blue
★	3782	◹	899	beige grey
⊟	3799		236	dk grey
⊙	310			black French Knot
▢	Green area indicates first row of right section of design.			

The design was stitched over 2 fabric threads on a 24" x 17" piece of Cream Lugana (25 ct). Three strands of floss were used for Cross Stitch and 1 strand for Half Cross Stitch, Backstitch, and French Knots. It was custom framed.

Design by Shirley Wilson.
Needlework adaptation by Jane Chandler.

33

For Sentimental Reasons

We cherish our favorite teddies for sentimental reasons — usually each one reminds us of someone we hold dear or of a day that's linked to loving memories. This collection honors those emotions and experiences that make our lives more fulfilling. In this sweet design, a wagonload of cubs portrays a timeless message about a mother's love.

...our love will pull us through...

94w x 75h

The design was stitched on a 14" x 13" piece of Ivory Aida (14 ct). Three strands of floss were used for Cross Stitch and 1 strand for Backstitch and French Knots. If desired, sew a 1¹⁄₈" dia. black button on top of wheel. It was made into a pillow.

For pillow, trim stitched piece 1¹⁄₄" larger on all sides than design. Cut one piece of fabric same size as stitched piece for backing.

For ruffle, press short ends of a 5" x 56" strip of fabric ¹⁄₂" to wrong side. Matching wrong sides and long edges, fold strip in half; press. Gather fabric strip to fit pillow. Matching raw edges and beginning at bottom edge, pin ruffle to right side of stitched piece, overlapping short ends ¹⁄₄"; use a ¹⁄₂" seam allowance to baste ruffle to stitched piece. Matching right sides and leaving an opening for turning, use a ¹⁄₂" seam allowance and sew stitched piece and backing fabric together. Trim corners diagonally. Turn pillow right side out, carefully pushing corners outward. Stuff pillow with polyester fiberfill and sew final closure by hand.

Design by Kathie Rueger.

X	DMC	¹⁄₄X	B'ST	ANC.	COLOR
•	blanc			2	white
O	ecru			387	ecru
●	310	◢	╱	403	black
✕	347	◢		1025	red
✦	434	◢		310	dk brown
◉	435	◢		1046	brown
✳	436	◢		1045	lt brown
S	561			212	green
C	738	◢		361	vy lt brown
☆	760			1022	dk pink
V	761			1021	pink
■	816	◢		1005	dk red
▨	898	◢	╱	360	vy dk brown
★	931	◢		1034	dk blue
2	932	◢		1033	blue
✵	3328	◢		1024	lt red
⊙	310	black French Knot			

A TRUE FRIEND

It's often said that a true friend is one who knows everything about you — and likes you anyway! This insightful design will make a sweet token of affection for someone who's been a blessing to you.

The design was stitched on an 11" x 9" piece of Ivory Aida (14 ct). Two strands of floss were used for Cross Stitch and 1 strand for Backstitch and French Knots. It was inserted in a mini towel rack frame (6¾" x 4½" opening).

Design by Debra Jordan Meyer for Fraser & Co.

X	DMC	¼X	B'ST	ANC.	COLOR
•	ecru			387	ecru
U	415			398	grey
•	434			310	dk tan
X	435			1046	tan
C	436			1045	lt tan
5	502			877	green
•	503			876	lt green
V	504			1042	vy lt green
–	738			361	vy lt tan
4	754			1012	peach
•	758			882	dk peach
•	760			1022	rose
△	761			1021	lt rose
P	842			388	beige
H	931			1034	blue
O	932			1033	lt blue
2	976			1001	copper
•	977			1002	lt copper
+	3024			397	taupe
▲	3328			1024	dk rose
◆	3371		✓	382	brown
•	503		lt green French Knot
•	3371		brown French Knot

58w x 50h

Share a little sunshine with someone who's touched your life by presenting them with this heartwarming design. The sincere message is sure to brighten their day!

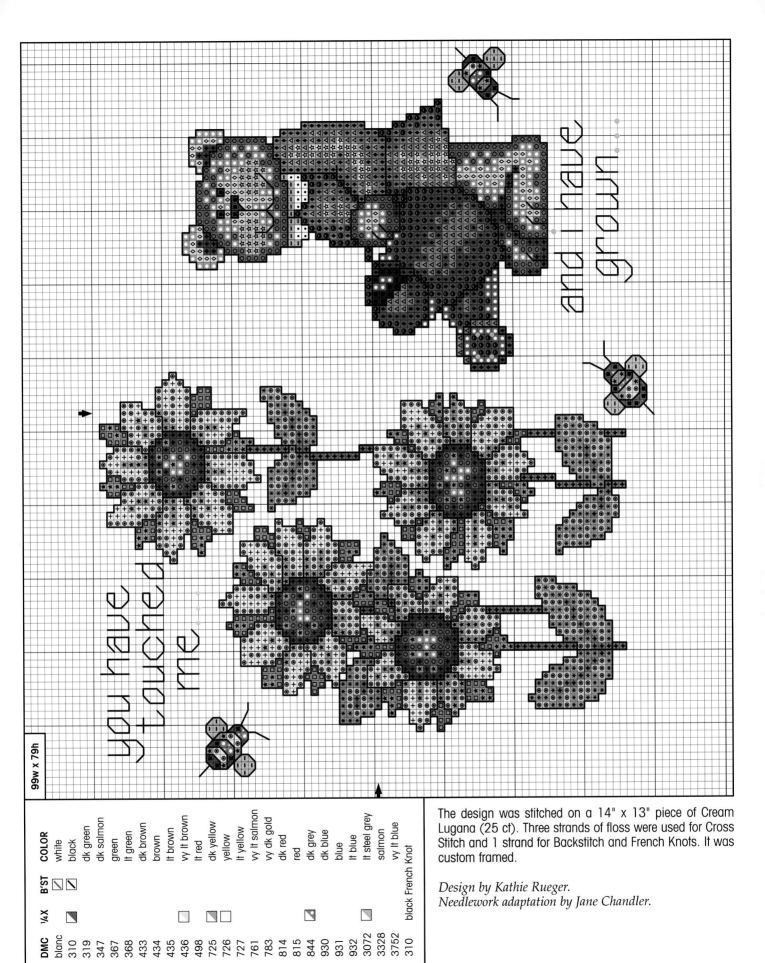

The design was stitched on a 14" x 13" piece of Cream Lugana (25 ct). Three strands of floss were used for Cross Stitch and 1 strand for Backstitch and French Knots. It was custom framed.

Design by Kathie Rueger.
Needlework adaptation by Jane Chandler.

X	DMC	¼X	B'ST	COLOR
•	blanc			white
■	310	◥	◩	black
★	319		◩	dk green
◆	347			dk salmon
✳	367			green
◉	368			lt green
✴	433			dk brown
○	434			brown
◉	435	▢		lt brown
◇	436	◪		vy lt brown
◐	498			lt red
★	725			dk yellow
◉	726			yellow
+	727			lt yellow
✩	761	◪		vy lt salmon
▢	783			vy dk gold
■	814			dk red
○	815			red
◑	844			dk grey
◆	930			dk blue
◁	931			blue
I	932	◪		lt blue
✩	3072			lt steel grey
☆	3328			salmon
◉	3752			vy lt blue
	310			black French Knot

99w x 79h

39

Touching moments like a big bear hug from Mom and a game of "ride the horsey" with Dad are what make parents dear to us. These unforgettable scenes are captured on mugs that let parents know they're the best!

54w x 44h

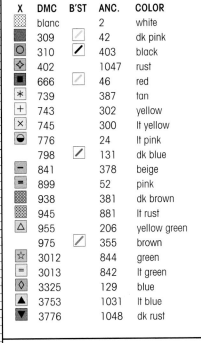

X	DMC	B'ST	ANC.	COLOR
▒	blanc		2	white
■	309	/	42	dk pink
○	310	/	403	black
◇	402		1047	rust
■	666	/	46	red
*	739		387	tan
+	743		302	yellow
×	745		300	lt yellow
◖	776		24	lt pink
	798	/	131	dk blue
−	841		378	beige
=	899		52	pink
▦	938		381	dk brown
▨	945		881	lt rust
△	955		206	yellow green
	975	/	355	brown
☆	3012		844	green
=	3013		842	lt green
◇	3325		129	blue
▲	3753		1031	lt blue
▼	3776		1048	dk rust

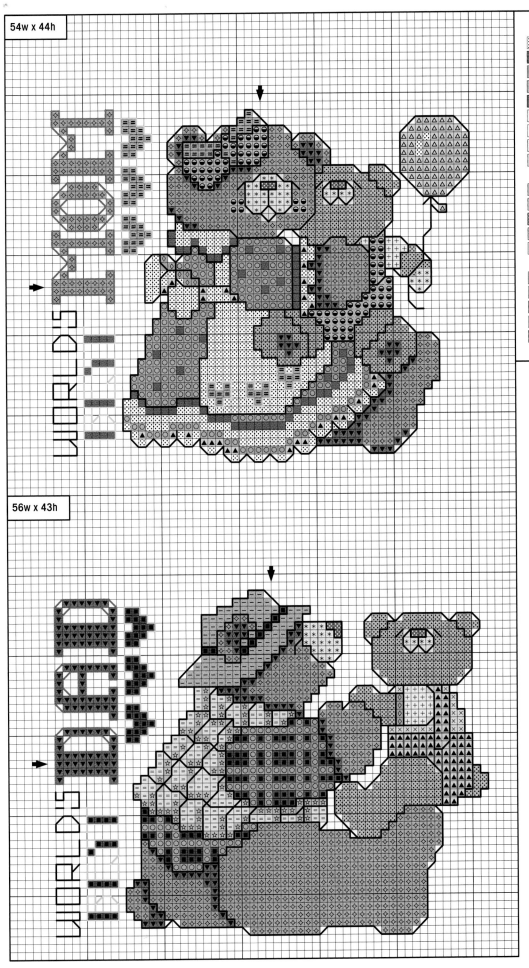

56w x 43h

Each design was stitched on a 10¼" x 3½" piece of Vinyl-Weave™ (14 ct). Three strands of floss were used for Cross Stitch and 1 strand for Backstitch. They were inserted in white mugs.

For design placement, fold vinyl in half, matching short edges. Center design on right half of vinyl if mug is to be used by a right-handed person or on the left half if mug is to be used by a left-handed person. Hand wash mug to protect stitchery.

Design by Linda Gillum.

AFTERNOON TEA

This timeless scene brings to mind the childhood tea parties we shared with teddy bears and dolls.

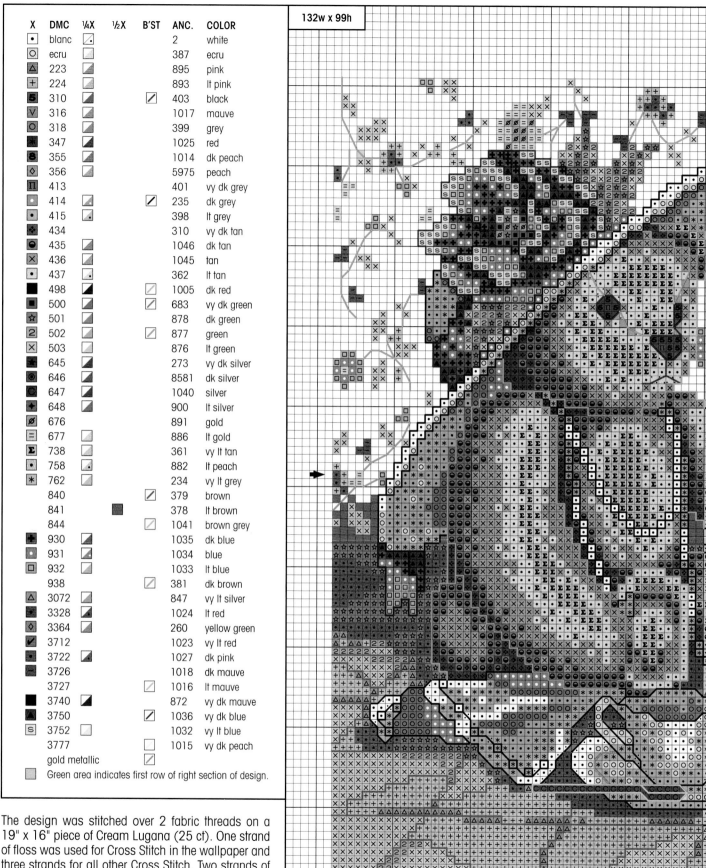

X	DMC	¼X	½X	B'ST	ANC.	COLOR
•	blanc				2	white
O	ecru				387	ecru
△	223				895	pink
+	224				893	lt pink
5	310			✓	403	black
V	316				1017	mauve
O	318				399	grey
✻	347				1025	red
8	355				1014	dk peach
◇	356				5975	peach
∏	413				401	vy dk grey
·	414			✓	235	dk grey
·	415				398	lt grey
✻	434				310	vy dk tan
⊙	435				1046	dk tan
✕	436				1045	tan
•	437				362	lt tan
■	498			✓	1005	dk red
■	500			✓	683	vy dk green
☆	501				878	dk green
2	502			✓	877	green
✕	503				876	lt green
✱	645				273	vy dk silver
◉	646				8581	dk silver
C	647				1040	silver
✦	648				900	lt silver
∅	676				891	gold
=	677				886	lt gold
Σ	738				361	vy lt tan
•	758				882	lt peach
✳	762				234	vy lt grey
	840			✓	379	brown
	841		■		378	lt brown
	844			✓	1041	brown grey
	938			✓	381	dk brown
△	3072				847	vy lt silver
■	3328				1024	lt red
◇	3364				260	yellow green
✔	3712				1023	vy lt red
•	3722				1027	dk pink
▨	3726				1018	dk mauve
	3727			✓	1016	lt mauve
■	3740				872	vy dk mauve
▲	3750			✓	1036	vy dk blue
S	3752				1032	vy lt blue
	3777				1015	vy dk peach
	gold metallic			✓		
	930				1035	dk blue
	931				1034	blue
	932				1033	lt blue

Green area indicates first row of right section of design.

132w x 99h

The design was stitched over 2 fabric threads on a 19" x 16" piece of Cream Lugana (25 ct). One strand of floss was used for Cross Stitch in the wallpaper and three strands for all other Cross Stitch. Two strands of floss were used for lt mauve Backstitch and 1 strand for all other Backstitch and Half Cross Stitch. It was custom framed.

Design by Donna Richardson.

Like a cherished teddy bear, the lessons we learn in Sunday school stick with us for a lifetime. We share two of our favorite scriptures — and some lovable bears — in this inspirational pair of designs.

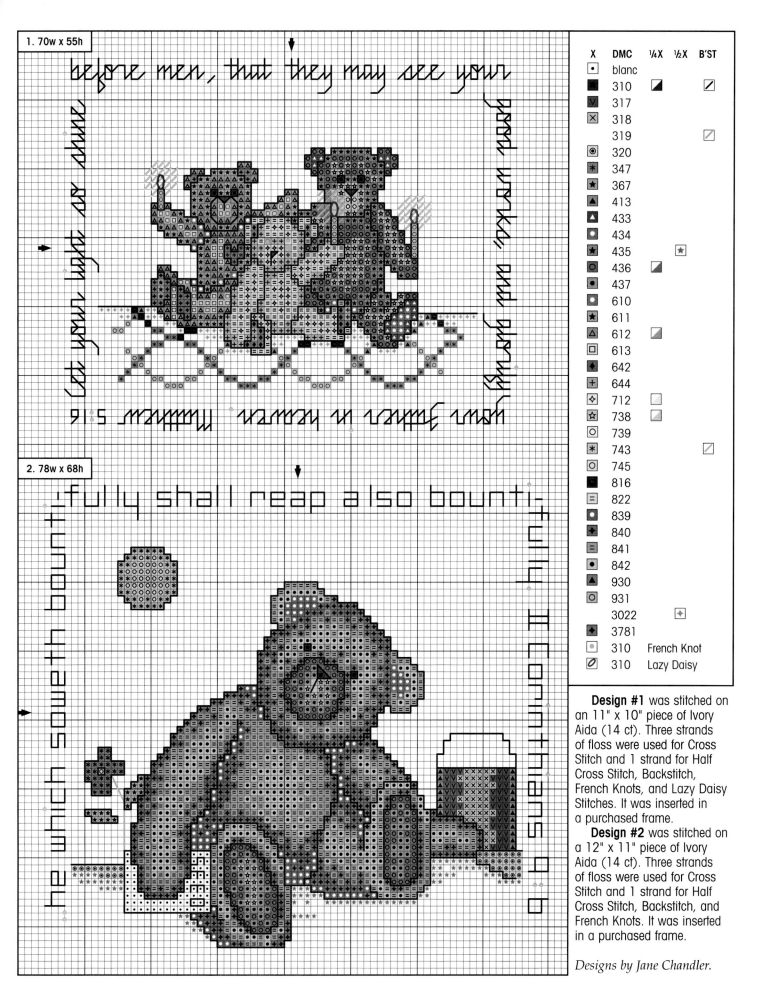

1. 70w x 55h

before men, that they may see your

2. 78w x 68h

fully shall reap also bounti-

X	DMC	¼X	½X	B'ST
·	blanc			
■	310	◢		◢
V	317			
✕	318			
	319			◢
◉	320			
✳	347			
★	367			
▲	413			
▲	433			
◎	434			
★	435		★	
◎	436	◢		
●	437			
◧	610			
★	611			
△	612	◢		
◻	613			
◆	642			
✚	644			
✦	712	◢		
☆	738	◢		
◯	739			
✳	743			◢
◯	745			
■	816			
▤	822			
◉	839			
✦	840			
▤	841			
●	842			
▲	930			
◎	931			
	3022		✦	
◆	3781			
◉	310	French Knot		
∅	310	Lazy Daisy		

Design #1 was stitched on an 11" x 10" piece of Ivory Aida (14 ct). Three strands of floss were used for Cross Stitch and 1 strand for Half Cross Stitch, Backstitch, French Knots, and Lazy Daisy Stitches. It was inserted in a purchased frame.

Design #2 was stitched on a 12" x 11" piece of Ivory Aida (14 ct). Three strands of floss were used for Cross Stitch and 1 strand for Half Cross Stitch, Backstitch, and French Knots. It was inserted in a purchased frame.

Designs by Jane Chandler.

The times we spend with friends and family in our homes are often some of the happiest moments in our lives. Displayed in your entryway, this cheery design will let special people know they're always welcome.

The design was stitched on a 15" x 13" piece of White Aida (14 ct). Three strands of floss were used for Cross Stitch and 1 strand for Backstitch. It was inserted in a purchased frame (10" x 8" opening).

Design by Kooler Design Studio.

127w x 98h

X	DMC	¼X	B'ST	
	blanc			
	310			*
	312			
	334			
	349			
	435			*
	436			
	676			
	721			†
	729			
	738			
	742			†
	772			†
	775			
	838			
	920			
	3325			
	3346			
	3347			
	3608			

* 310 for eyes and 721 for border.
† 742 for border, 920 for pineapples, and 838 for remaining backstitch.

Priscilla and her little friend Ben are all dressed up and ready for a day filled with adventure! The fun-loving twosome will look especially charming when paired with Kindred Spirits on page 52.

75w x 87h

X	DMC	¼X	½X	B'ST	COLOR
·	blanc				white
⊙	ecru	◹			ecru
	322			╱	dk blue
	347			╱	red
	367			╱	green
+	368	◹			lt green
◇	543				lt beige
⊠	611				dk tan
	646		■		dk grey
	648		■		grey
⊡	676	◹			gold

X	DMC	¼X	B'ST	COLOR
✳	677			lt gold
C	680			lt brown
☆	729			dk gold
◆	760		╱ *	dk pink
●	761	◹		pink
▢	775			vy lt blue
	840		╱	beige
	869		╱	brown
★	3031	◹		dk brown
★	3032			tan
×	3033	◹		vy lt tan

X	DMC	¼X	B'ST	COLOR
▽	3325			lt blue
⊓	3712			vy dk pink
◉	3713			lt pink
−	3755			blue
	3781		╱	vy dk tan
△	3782	◹		lt tan
·	blanc		white French Knot
●	745		yellow French Knot
⊘	3325		lt blue Lazy Daisy Stitch
* Use 2 strands of floss.			

The design was stitched over 2 fabric threads on a 14" x 15" piece of Cream Lugana (25 ct). Three strands of floss were used for Cross Stitch, 2 strands for Lazy Daisy Stitches, and 1 strand for Backstitch and French Knots, unless otherwise noted in color key. It was custom framed.

Design by Mary King. Needlework adaptation by Jane Chandler.

51

Sometimes unlikely companions, such as Drusilla the bear and Goldie the goose, make the best of friends. This portrait of kindred spirits makes a sweet complement to display with "Beary" Best Friends *on page 50.*

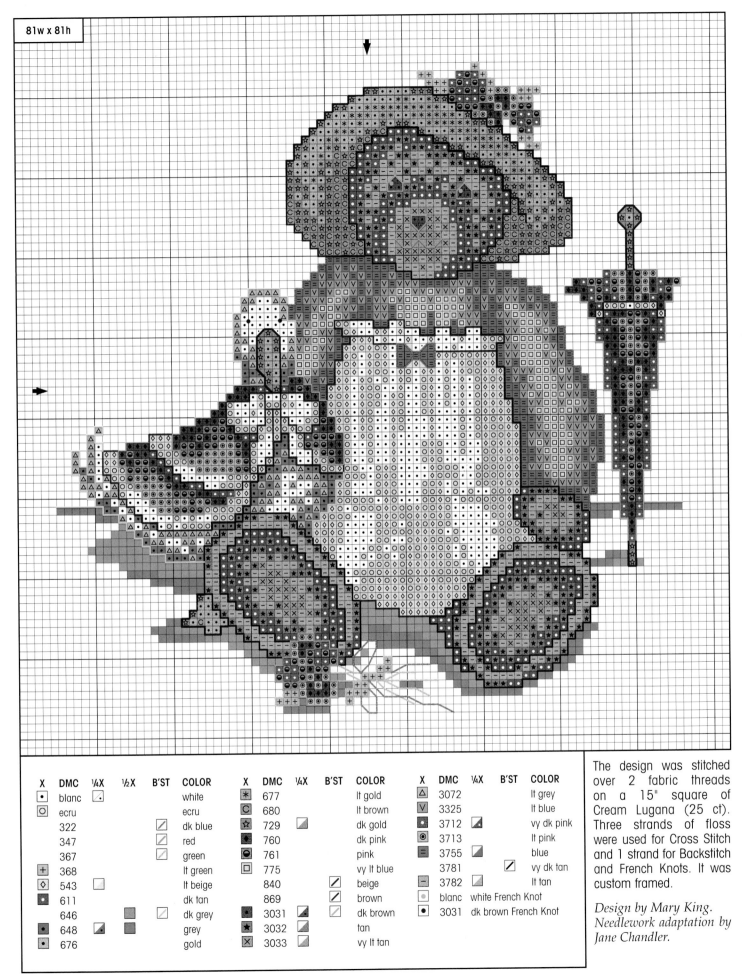

81w x 81h

X	DMC	¼X	½X	B'ST	COLOR
•	blanc				white
⊙	ecru				ecru
	322			╱	dk blue
	347			╱	red
	367			╱	green
+	368				lt green
◇	543				lt beige
▨	611				dk tan
	646		▨	╱	dk grey
◈	648	◪	▨		grey
•	676				gold

X	DMC	¼X	B'ST	COLOR
✳	677			lt gold
C	680			lt brown
☆	729	◪		dk gold
◆	760			dk pink
◉	761			pink
▢	775			vy lt blue
	840		╱	beige
	869		╱	brown
▨	3031	◪	╱	dk brown
★	3032	◪		tan
✕	3033	◪		vy lt tan

X	DMC	¼X	B'ST	COLOR
△	3072			lt grey
V	3325			lt blue
▨	3712	◪		vy dk pink
◉	3713			lt pink
▬	3755	◪		blue
	3781		╱	vy dk tan
▬	3782	◪		lt tan
●	blanc			white French Knot
●	3031			dk brown French Knot

The design was stitched over 2 fabric threads on a 15" square of Cream Lugana (25 ct). Three strands of floss were used for Cross Stitch and 1 strand for Backstitch and French Knots. It was custom framed.

Design by Mary King. Needlework adaptation by Jane Chandler.

Love-worn teddy bears, quilts, and little red wagons are always in the picture when we make a list of our favorite things.

X	DMC	¼X	½X	B'ST	COLOR	X	DMC	¼X	COLOR	X	DMC	¼X	COLOR
●	310	◪		◢	black	−	500		green	+	841	◪	beige
■	321				red	★	642		tan	●	842		lt beige
▼	336				blue	●	644	◪	lt tan	2	902		dk maroon
◆	414				dk grey brown	○	739		vy lt beige	S	3022		grey brown
◑	434		◪		dk gold	+	814		maroon	Σ	3023		lt grey brown
✤	435		■		gold	◉	816		lt maroon	☆	3024	◪	vy lt grey brown
◆	436				lt gold	▲	839		vy dk beige	C	3790		dk tan
✕	437		■		vy lt gold	◆	840		dk beige	●	310		black French Knot

The design was stitched on a 16" square of Ivory Aida (14 ct). Three strands of floss were used for Cross Stitch and 1 strand for Half Cross Stitch, Backstitch, and French Knots. It was custom framed.

Design by Jane Chandler.

Little Teddy Bears

Children are "beary" special people — they fill our hearts with love and give our lives a sense of continued joy. These precious gifts from God are sweetly remembered in this touching collection. You'll find lots of treasures for baby, from afghans and bibs to a birth sampler and sipper cups. As your little ones grow, our Look What I Did! design will let you proudly display their artwork or school papers. What a great way to nurture self-esteem!

The design was stitched on a 13" x 11" piece of White Aida (14 ct). Three strands of floss were used for Cross Stitch and 1 strand for Backstitch. It was inserted in a purchased frame (5" x 7" opening). Refer to photo to glue two 45mm spring clothespins to frame.

Design by Linda Gillum.

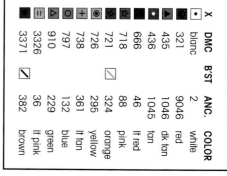

X	B'ST	DMC	ANC.	COLOR
▪		blanc	2	white
◫		321	9046	red
▷		435	1046	dk tan
◻		436	1045	tan
◯		666	46	lt red
➕		718	88	pink
◉		721	324	orange
✳		726	295	yellow
✴		738	361	lt tan
▪		797	132	blue
◦		910	229	green
▪	◹	3326	36	lt pink
◻	◹	3371	382	brown

92w x 64h

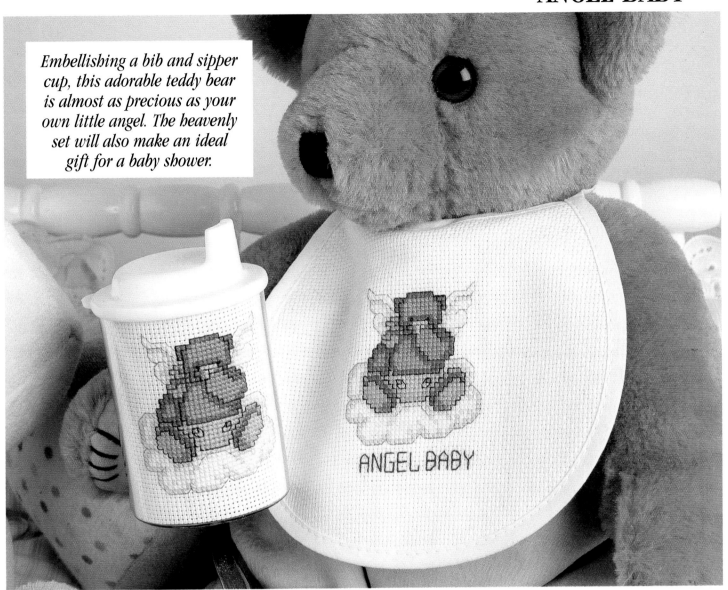

Embellishing a bib and sipper cup, this adorable teddy bear is almost as precious as your own little angel. The heavenly set will also make an ideal gift for a baby shower.

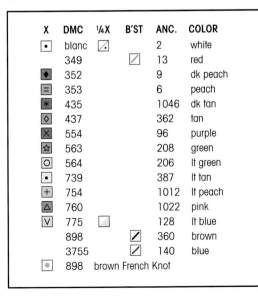

X	DMC	¼X	B'ST	ANC.	COLOR
•	blanc	◿		2	white
	349		◿	13	red
◆	352			9	dk peach
⊟	353			6	peach
✳	435			1046	dk tan
◇	437			362	tan
✕	554			96	purple
☆	563			208	green
○	564			206	lt green
•	739			387	lt tan
+	754			1012	lt peach
△	760			1022	pink
V	775	◻		128	lt blue
	898		◿	360	brown
	3755		◿	140	blue
⊙	898		brown French Knot		

Design by Lorri Birmingham.

32w x 41h

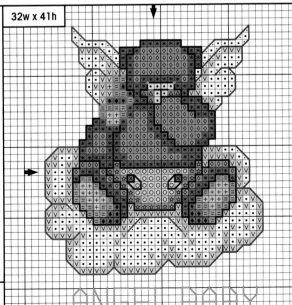

The entire design was centered and stitched on a white Aida (14 ct) baby bib. Three strands of floss were used for Cross Stitch and 1 strand for Backstitch and French Knots.

Baby and Cloud only were stitched (omitting Quarter Stitches) on a 7½" x 3" piece of Vinyl-Weave™ (14 ct). Three strands of floss were used for Cross Stitch and 1 strand for Backstitch and French Knots. It was inserted in a Stitch-A-Sipper™. Hand wash to protect stitchery.

Anyone who loves children will be inspired by these "beary" gentle proverbs. Displayed in a frame, the lessons of love will provide a daily reminder of how important it is to guide and cherish our children.

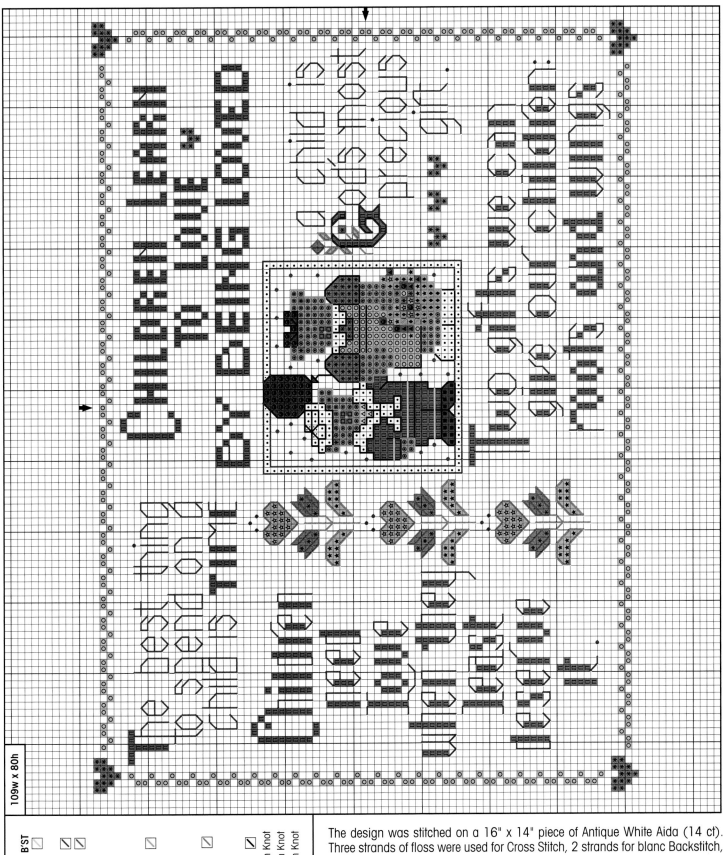

The design was stitched on a 16" x 14" piece of Antique White Aida (14 ct). Three strands of floss were used for Cross Stitch, 2 strands for blanc Backstitch, and 1 strand for all other Backstitch and French Knots. It was custom framed.

Design by Nancy Rossi.

Rock your little one to sleep wrapped in one of these sweet afghans featuring boy and girl bears. You'll want to make a matching pillow, too.

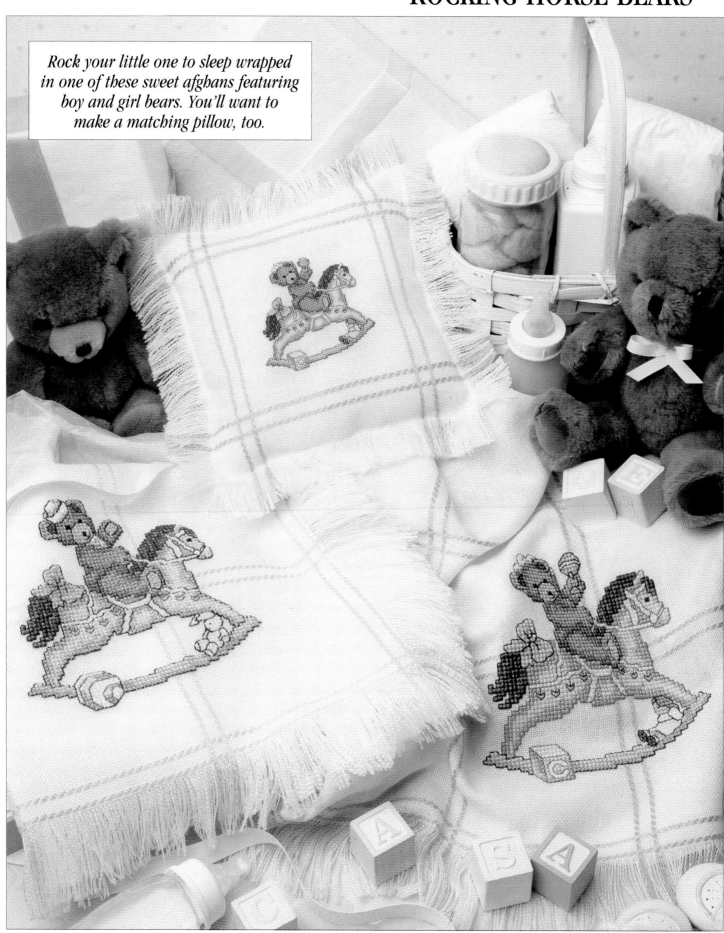

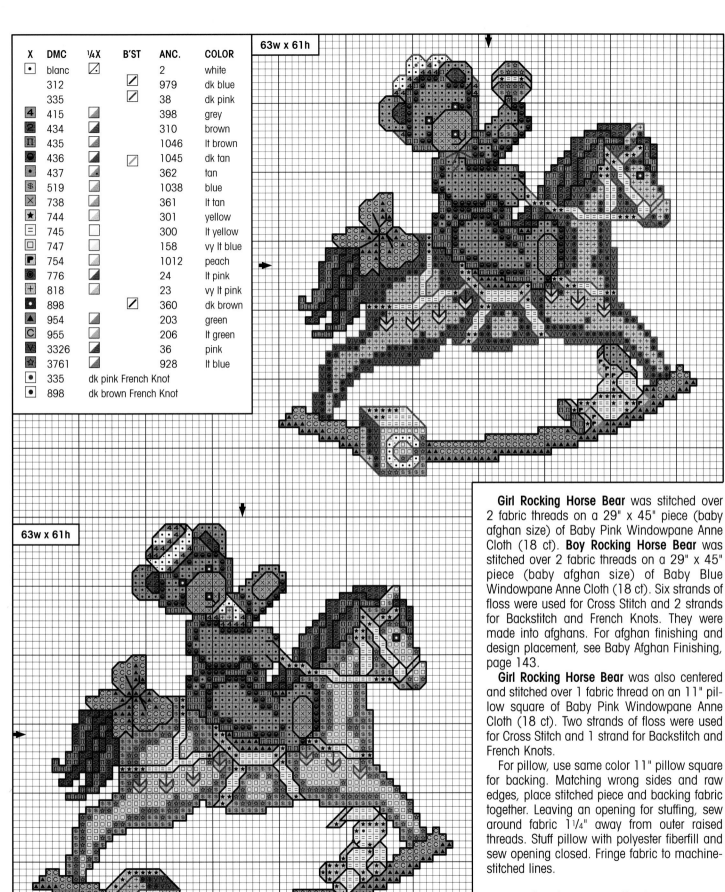

X	DMC	1/4X	B'ST	ANC.	COLOR
•	blanc	◩		2	white
	312		◪	979	dk blue
	335		◪	38	dk pink
4	415	◪		398	grey
2	434	◪		310	brown
Π	435	◪		1046	lt brown
◉	436	◪	◪	1045	dk tan
•	437	◪		362	tan
$	519	◪		1038	blue
X	738	◪		361	lt tan
★	744	◪		301	yellow
=	745	☐		300	lt yellow
▢	747	☐		158	vy lt blue
▣	754	◪		1012	peach
◎	776	◪		24	lt pink
+	818	◪		23	vy lt pink
◙	898		◪	360	dk brown
▲	954	◪		203	green
C	955	◪		206	lt green
V	3326	◪		36	pink
☆	3761	◪		928	lt blue
•	335				dk pink French Knot
•	898				dk brown French Knot

63w x 61h

63w x 61h

Girl Rocking Horse Bear was stitched over 2 fabric threads on a 29" x 45" piece (baby afghan size) of Baby Pink Windowpane Anne Cloth (18 ct). **Boy Rocking Horse Bear** was stitched over 2 fabric threads on a 29" x 45" piece (baby afghan size) of Baby Blue Windowpane Anne Cloth (18 ct). Six strands of floss were used for Cross Stitch and 2 strands for Backstitch and French Knots. They were made into afghans. For afghan finishing and design placement, see Baby Afghan Finishing, page 143.

Girl Rocking Horse Bear was also centered and stitched over 1 fabric thread on an 11" pillow square of Baby Pink Windowpane Anne Cloth (18 ct). Two strands of floss were used for Cross Stitch and 1 strand for Backstitch and French Knots.

For pillow, use same color 11" pillow square for backing. Matching wrong sides and raw edges, place stitched piece and backing fabric together. Leaving an opening for stuffing, sew around fabric 1¼" away from outer raised threads. Stuff pillow with polyester fiberfill and sew opening closed. Fringe fabric to machine-stitched lines.

Designs by The Fraser Collection.

the fraser collection

Score a touchdown with your little football fan when you present him with this terrific tee! Wearing our geared-up bear, he'll be ready to tackle the world.

66w x 77h

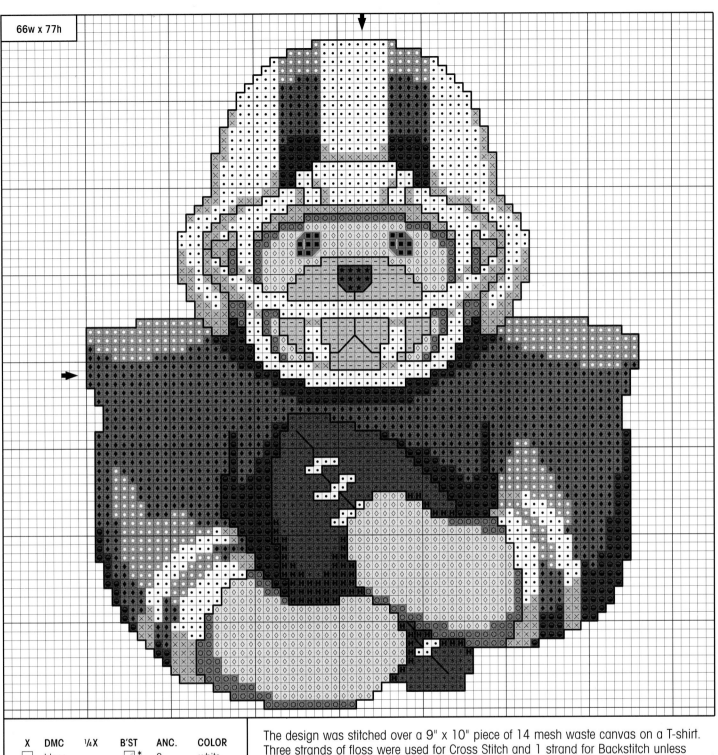

X	DMC	¼X	B'ST	ANC.	COLOR
•	blanc		◿*	2	white
■	300			352	dk rust
✖	301			1049	rust
■	310	◿	◿	403	black
◆	321			9046	red
✕	415			398	grey
✦	433	◿		358	brown
◎	435			1046	lt brown
◇	437	◻		362	tan
◼	498			1005	dk red
◙	666			46	lt red
-	739	◿		387	lt tan
	938		◿	381	dk brown
*	Use 2 strands of floss.				

The design was stitched over a 9" x 10" piece of 14 mesh waste canvas on a T-shirt. Three strands of floss were used for Cross Stitch and 1 strand for Backstitch unless otherwise noted in color key. See Working on Waste Canvas, page 143.

Design by Holly DeFount.

With their high energy and enthusiasm, children make natural cheerleaders. A purchased dress stitched with our exuberant bear will encourage your little miss to excel at any activity.

90w x 85h

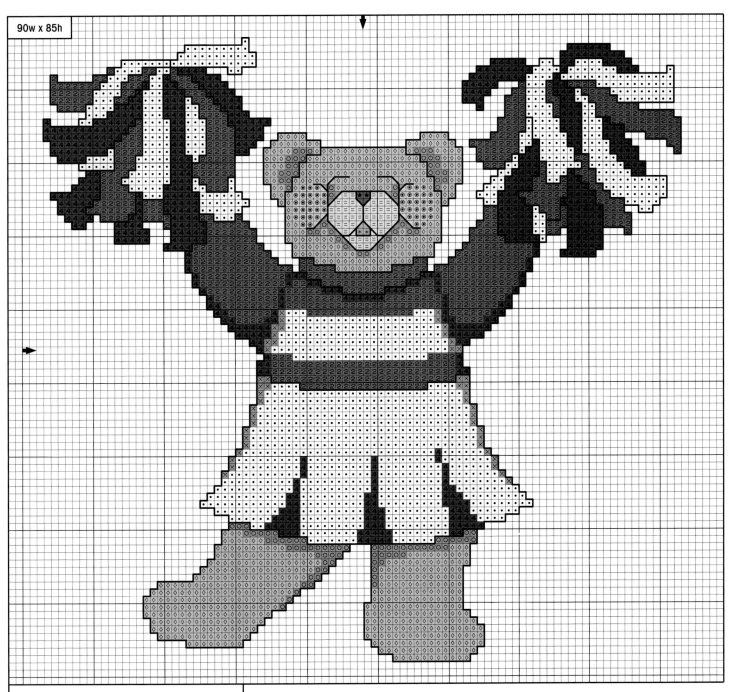

X	DMC	¼X	B'ST	ANC.	COLOR
•	blanc			2	white
▲	208			110	dk lavender
2	210			108	lavender
✕	415			398	lt grey
★	433	◢		358	dk brown
◉	435	◢		1046	brown
◇	437			362	tan
=	739	◢		387	lt tan
	938		◢	381	vy dk brown
✳	957	◢		50	rose
◉	963	◢		73	lt rose

The design was stitched over an 11" x 10" piece of 14 mesh waste canvas on a dress. Three strands of floss were used for Cross Stitch and 1 strand for Backstitch. See Working on Waste Canvas, page 143.

Design by Holly DeFount.

This whimsical birth sampler is as simple to make as A-B-C. And who better than a lovable, huggable teddy to announce baby's arrival!

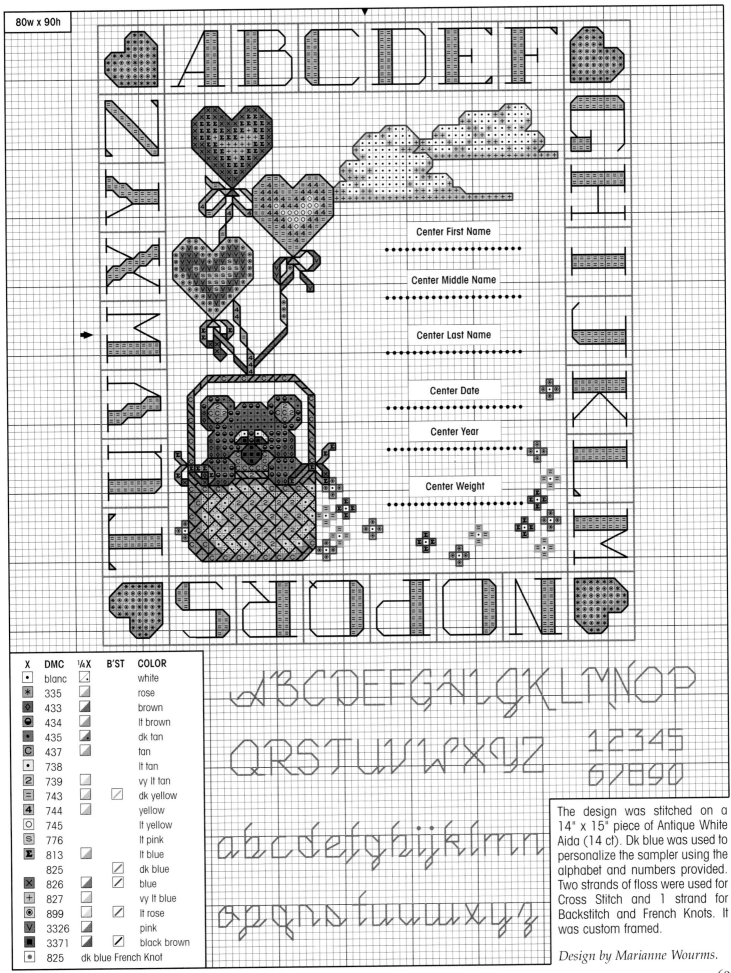

80w x 90h

Center First Name

Center Middle Name

Center Last Name

Center Date

Center Year

Center Weight

X	DMC	¼X	B'ST	COLOR
•	blanc			white
*	335			rose
◈	433			brown
◓	434			lt brown
⬙	435			dk tan
C	437			tan
•	738			lt tan
2	739			vy lt tan
꞊	743		╱	dk yellow
4	744			yellow
O	745			lt yellow
S	776			lt pink
Σ	813			lt blue
	825		╱	dk blue
X	826		╱	blue
+	827			vy lt blue
◉	899		╱	lt rose
V	3326			pink
■	3371		╱	black brown
•	825			dk blue French Knot

The design was stitched on a 14" x 15" piece of Antique White Aida (14 ct). Dk blue was used to personalize the sampler using the alphabet and numbers provided. Two strands of floss were used for Cross Stitch and 1 strand for Backstitch and French Knots. It was custom framed.

Design by Marianne Wourms.

BABY'S DREAM BOAT

Reminiscent of a fairy tale, this exquisite illustration showcases a baby teddy bear sailing through a sea of clouds. The enchanting afghan and framed piece will bring the magic of make-believe to life for you and a little one.

91w x 135h

The entire design was stitched over 2 fabric threads on a 17" x 20" piece of Antique White Lugana (25 ct). Three strands of floss were used for Cross Stitch and 1 strand for Half Cross Stitch, Backstitch, French Knots, and Lazy Daisy Stitches. It was custom framed.

A portion of the design (refer to photo) was stitched over 2 fabric threads on a 29" x 45" piece (baby afghan size) of White All-Cotton Anne Cloth (18 ct). Six strands of floss were used for Cross Stitch and 2 strands for Backstitch, French Knots, and Lazy Daisy Stitches. It was made into an afghan. Refer to Diagram for placement of design on fabric.

X	DMC	ANC.	COLOR	½X	¼X	B'ST
	blanc	2	white			
	ecru	387	ecru			
	208	110	dk purple			
	209	109	purple			
	210	108	lt purple			
	211	342	vy lt purple			
	310	403	black			◥
	335	38	dk pink			◥
	415	398	grey			
	433	358	dk brown			◥
	434	310	brown			
	435	1046	lt brown			
	437	362	dk tan			
	519	1038	blue green			

X	DMC	ANC.	COLOR	¼X	B'ST
	543	933	cream		
	645	273	beige grey		
	738	361	tan		
	739	387	lt tan		
	742	303	dk orange		
	743	302	dk yellow		
	744	301	yellow		
	762	234	lt grey		
	775	128	lt blue		
	776	24	lt pink		
	818	23	vy lt pink		
	844	1041	dk beige grey		
	899	52	pink		
	910	229	dk green		◥

X	DMC	ANC.	COLOR	¼X	B'ST
	913	204	green		
	958	187	dk aqua		
	959	186	aqua		
	964	185	lt aqua		
	3024	397	lt beige grey		
	3755	140	blue		◥
	3821		gold		
	3822		lt gold		
	3823		lt yellow		

blanc — white French Knot
910 — dk green Lazy Daisy Stitch

Grey area indicates last row of top section of design.

For afghan, cut selvages from fabric. Machine stitch along raised threads around outside edge of afghan. Fringe fabric to machine-stitched lines.

Design by Carol Bryan.
Needlework adaptation by Jane Chandler.

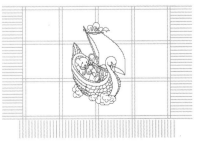

73

Tenderhearted teddy bears make wonderful companions for even the smallest of children. These designs add playful touches to accessories for baby, including an afghan, a bib, a mug, and a sweatshirt.

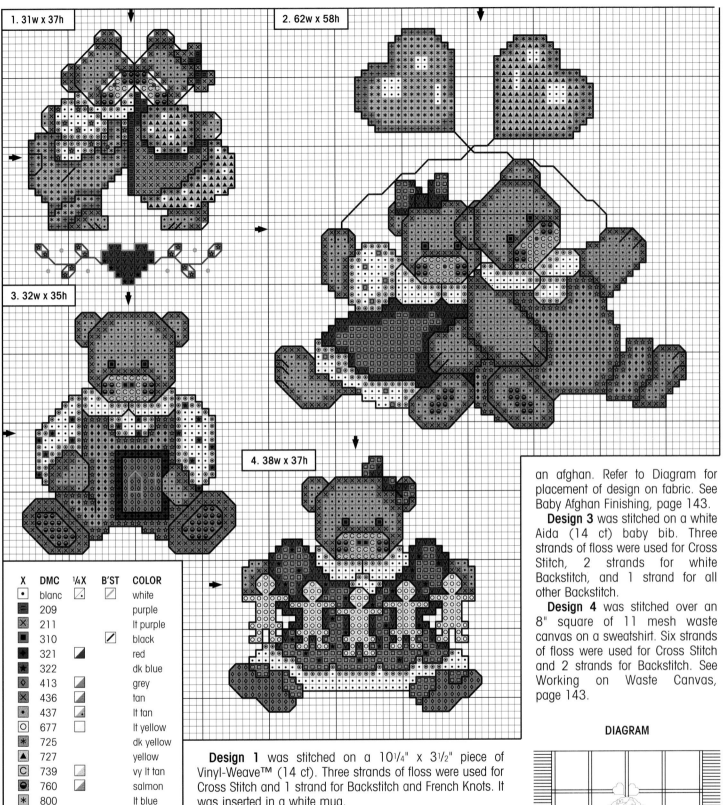

1. 31w x 37h

2. 62w x 58h

3. 32w x 35h

4. 38w x 37h

X	DMC	¼X	B'ST	COLOR
•	blanc			white
■	209			purple
✕	211			lt purple
■	310		/	black
■	321	◪		red
★	322			dk blue
◆	413	◪		grey
✕	436	◪		tan
•	437	◪	◢	lt tan
○	677	□		lt yellow
✳	725			dk yellow
▲	727			yellow
C	739	◪		vy lt tan
◒	760	◪		salmon
✳	800			lt blue
✚	809			blue
★	899		◪	dk rose
☆	954	◪	/	green
◆	955			lt green
□	963			lt rose
▼	3326	◪		rose
◉	3753	□		vy lt blue
•	310			black French Knot
•	899			dk rose French Knot

Design 1 was stitched on a 10¼" x 3½" piece of Vinyl-Weave™ (14 ct). Three strands of floss were used for Cross Stitch and 1 strand for Backstitch and French Knots. It was inserted in a white mug.

For design placement, fold vinyl in half, matching short edges. Center design on right half of vinyl if mug is to be used by a right-handed person or on the left half if mug is to be used by a left-handed person. Hand wash mug to protect stitchery.

Design 2 was stitched over 2 fabric threads on a 29" x 45" piece (baby afghan size) of Soft White Anne Cloth (18 ct). Six strands of floss were used for Cross Stitch and 2 strands for Backstitch and French Knots. It was made into

an afghan. Refer to Diagram for placement of design on fabric. See Baby Afghan Finishing, page 143.

Design 3 was stitched on a white Aida (14 ct) baby bib. Three strands of floss were used for Cross Stitch, 2 strands for white Backstitch, and 1 strand for all other Backstitch.

Design 4 was stitched over an 8" square of 11 mesh waste canvas on a sweatshirt. Six strands of floss were used for Cross Stitch and 2 strands for Backstitch. See Working on Waste Canvas, page 143.

DIAGRAM

Designs by Lorraine Birmingham.

Handy for back-to-school, these nifty tote bags are just right for carrying a child's favorite things. The sturdy carryalls are sure to get high marks from your little student — especially when they're accented with one of our delightful designs for boys or girls.

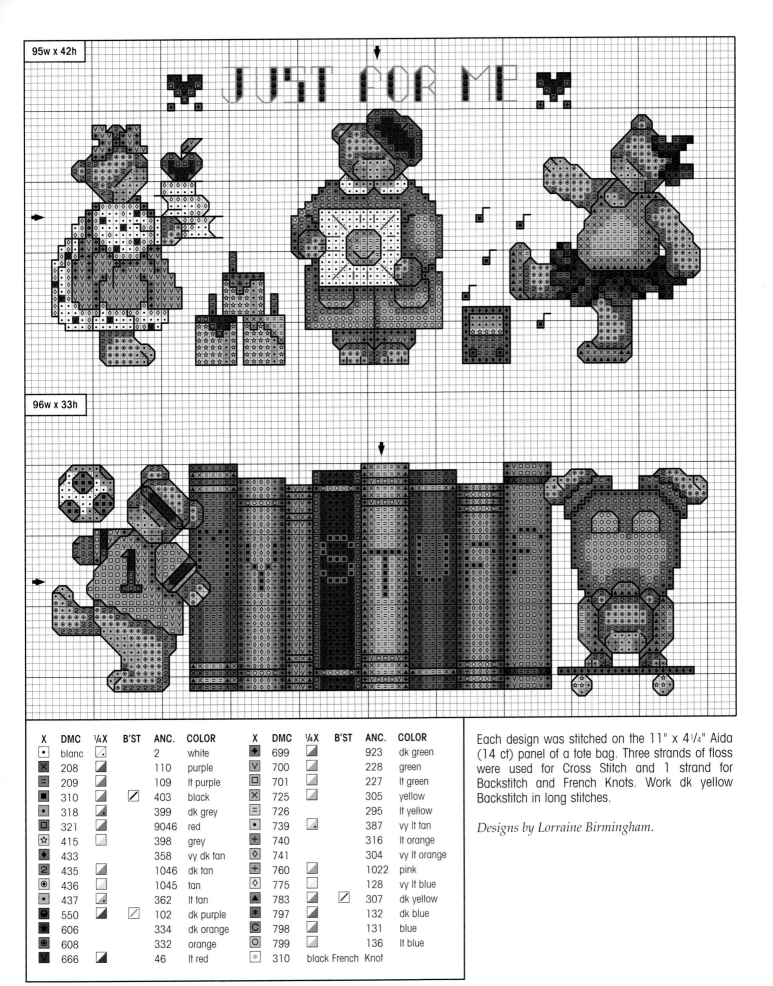

X	DMC	¼X	B'ST	ANC.	COLOR
·	blanc			2	white
X	208			110	purple
=	209			109	lt purple
■	310		✓	403	black
·	318			399	dk grey
□	321			9046	red
☆	415			398	grey
◆	433		✓	358	vy dk tan
2	435			1046	dk tan
◉	436			1045	tan
·	437			362	lt tan
◑	550			102	dk purple
★	606			334	dk orange
◎	608			332	orange
V	666			46	lt red

X	DMC	¼X	B'ST	ANC.	COLOR
✦	699			923	dk green
V	700			228	green
▣	701			227	lt green
X	725			305	yellow
=	726			295	lt yellow
·	739			387	vy lt tan
+	740			316	lt orange
◇	741			304	vy lt orange
+	760			1022	pink
◇	775			128	vy lt blue
▲	783		✓	307	dk yellow
✳	797			132	dk blue
C	798			131	blue
◎	799			136	lt blue
●	310			black French Knot	

Each design was stitched on the 11" x 4¼" Aida (14 ct) panel of a tote bag. Three strands of floss were used for Cross Stitch and 1 strand for Backstitch and French Knots. Work dk yellow Backstitch in long stitches.

Designs by Lorraine Birmingham.

Want to add a bit of fun to baby's mealtime? This bib and towel set features a friendly panda before and after he's enjoyed his wagonload of fruits and vegetables.

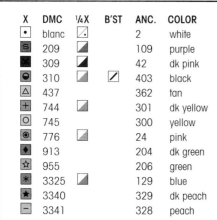

X	DMC	¼X	B'ST	ANC.	COLOR
•	blanc			2	white
S	209			109	purple
✕	309			42	dk pink
⊖	310		✓	403	black
△	437			362	tan
+	744			301	dk yellow
○	745			300	yellow
◉	776			24	pink
◆	913			204	dk green
☆	955			206	green
✳	3325			129	blue
★	3340			329	dk peach
−	3341			328	peach

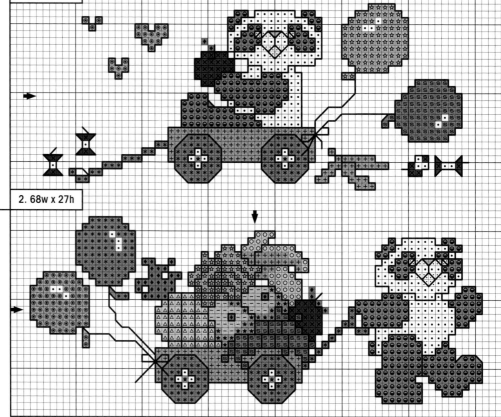

1. 64w x 27h

2. 68w x 27h

Design 1 was stitched on the 14 ct insert of a white fingertip towel. Three strands of floss were used for Cross Stitch and 1 strand for Backstitch.

Design 2 was stitched on the 14 ct insert of a white baby bib. Three strands of floss were used for Cross Stitch and 1 strand for Backstitch.

Designs by Linda Gillum.

Playfully posed on blocks that spell out the word "Baby," these frolicking cubs make a sweet design for the nursery.

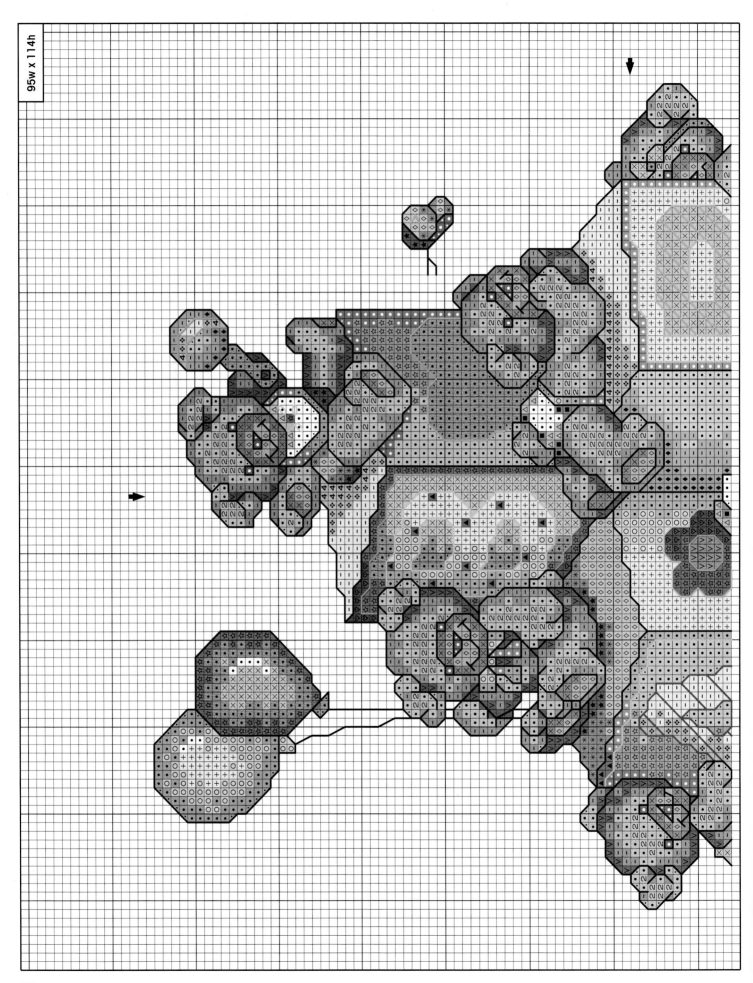

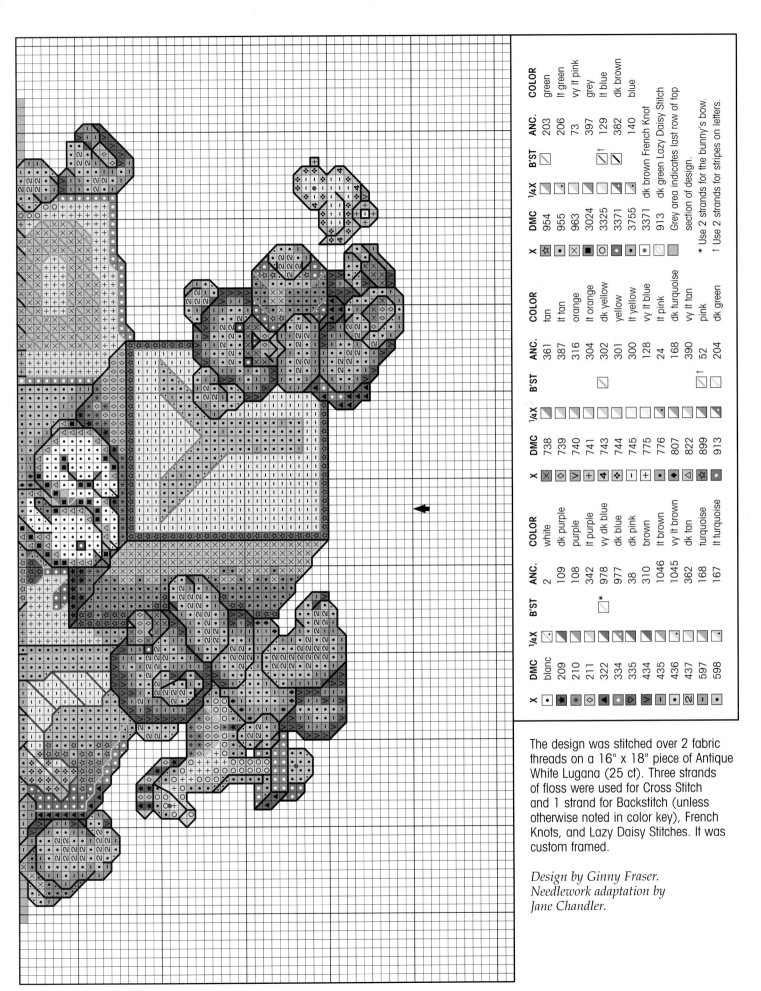

X	DMC	ANC.	1/4X	B'ST	COLOR
	954	203			green
	955	206			lt green
	963	73			vy lt pink
	3024	397			grey
	3325	129			lt blue
	3371	382			dk brown
	3755	140			blue
	3371				dk brown French Knot
	913				dk green Lazy Daisy Stitch

Grey area indicates last row of top section of design.

* Use 2 strands for the bunny's bow.
† Use 2 strands for stripes on letters.

X	DMC	ANC.	1/4X	B'ST	COLOR
	738	361			tan
	739	387			lt tan
	740	316			orange
	741	304			lt orange
	743	302			dk yellow
	744	301			yellow
	745	300			lt yellow
	775	128			vy lt blue
	776	24			lt pink
	807	168			dk turquoise
	822	390			vy lt tan
	899	52			pink
	913	204			dk green

X	DMC	ANC.	1/4X	B'ST	COLOR
	blanc	2			white
	209	109			dk purple
	210	108			purple
	211	342			lt purple
	322	978			vy dk blue
	334	977			dk blue
	335	38			dk pink
	434	310			brown
	435	1046			lt brown
	436	1045			vy lt brown
	437	362			dk tan
	597	168			turquoise
	598	167			lt turquoise

The design was stitched over 2 fabric threads on a 16" x 18" piece of Antique White Lugana (25 ct). Three strands of floss were used for Cross Stitch and 1 strand for Backstitch (unless otherwise noted in color key), French Knots, and Lazy Daisy Stitches. It was custom framed.

Design by Ginny Fraser.
Needlework adaptation by
Jane Chandler.

Beary Happy Holidays

Celebrating the holidays is more fun when you share the time with friends. And who better than an old chum like Teddy to make special occasions merrier! This fun assortment of designs celebrates all our favorite holidays from Valentine's Day to Christmas. You'll find a variety of projects, too, such as ornaments, a sweater, a wall hanging, and more. An artistic bear dazzles us with his "sweet" designs on an afghan in Candy Cane Red.

Diagram

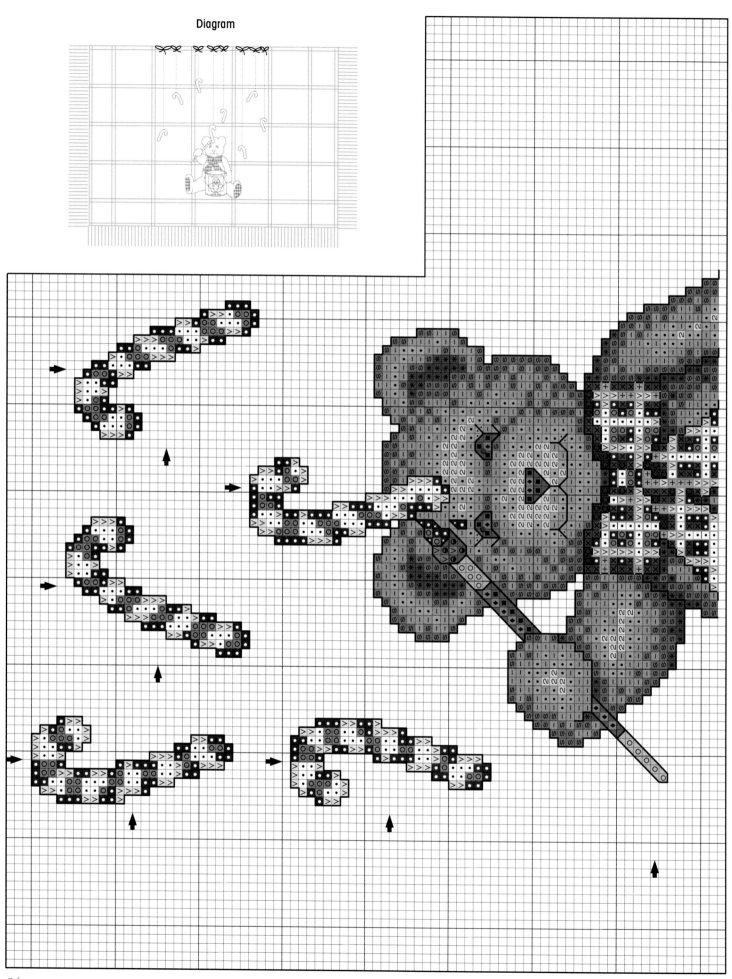

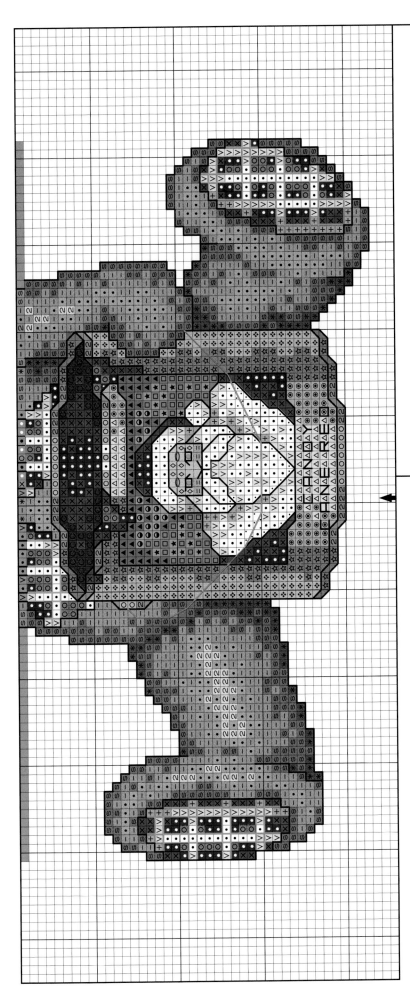

X	DMC	1/4X	B'ST	ANC.	COLOR
	739			387	vy lt tan
	754			1012	peach
	761			1021	pink
	783			307	vy dk gold
	815			43	vy dk red
	822			390	beige
	839			360	dk brown
	840			379	brown
	844			1041	vy dk grey
	991			189	dk green
	992			187	green
	3328			1024	lt red

Grey area indicates last row of top section of design.

	blanc	white French Knot
	336	dk blue French Knot
	blanc	white Lazy Daisy

X	DMC	1/4X	B'ST	ANC.	COLOR
	blanc			2	white
	310			403	black
	312			979	blue
	318			399	grey
	336			150	dk blue
	347			1025	red
	414			235	dk grey
	415			398	lt grey
	435			1046	vy dk tan
	436			1045	dk tan
	437			362	tan
	498			1005	dk red
	644			830	dk beige
	725			305	dk gold
	726			295	gold
	727			293	lt gold
	738			361	lt tan

The design was stitched over 2 fabric threads on a 45" x 58" piece (standard afghan size) of Bayberry Anne Cloth (18 ct). Six strands of floss were used for Cross Stitch and 2 strands for Backstitch, French Knots, and Lazy Daisy Stitches. It was made into an afghan. Refer to Diagram for placement of designs on fabric. See Afghan Finishing, page 143.

For each candy cane hanger, thread a 20" length of 1/16"w ribbon through a chenille needle. Referring to **Fig. 1** for placement, insert needle from right side of fabric at **A** and pull through leaving a 4" tail; bring needle back through to right side of fabric at **B**; tie tail and long end in a knot close to fabric. Use remaining ribbon to work Running Stitches (over 6 threads, under 2 threads) to desired point on afghan (see Diagram). Tack ribbon to wrong side of fabric. Tie a 5" length of ribbon in a bow; tack bow to top of ribbon. Trim all ribbon ends as desired and apply liquid fray preventative.

Fig. 1

Design by Jan Jameson for Heartprint Greeting Cards, Inc.
Needlework adaptation by Jane Chandler.

These matchmaking bears know that you shouldn't wear your heart on your sleeve — it belongs on the front of your sweater where everyone can see it! On Valentine's Day, this sweet design will let that special someone know you're feeling romantic.

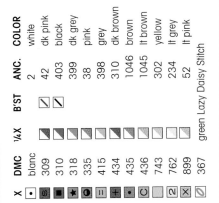

DMC	B'ST	¼X	X	ANC.	COLOR
blanc			·	2	white
309				42	dk pink
310				403	black
318				399	dk grey
335				38	pink
415				398	grey
434				310	dk brown
435				1046	brown
436				1045	lt brown
743				302	yellow
762				234	lt grey
899				52	lt pink
367					green Lazy Daisy Stitch

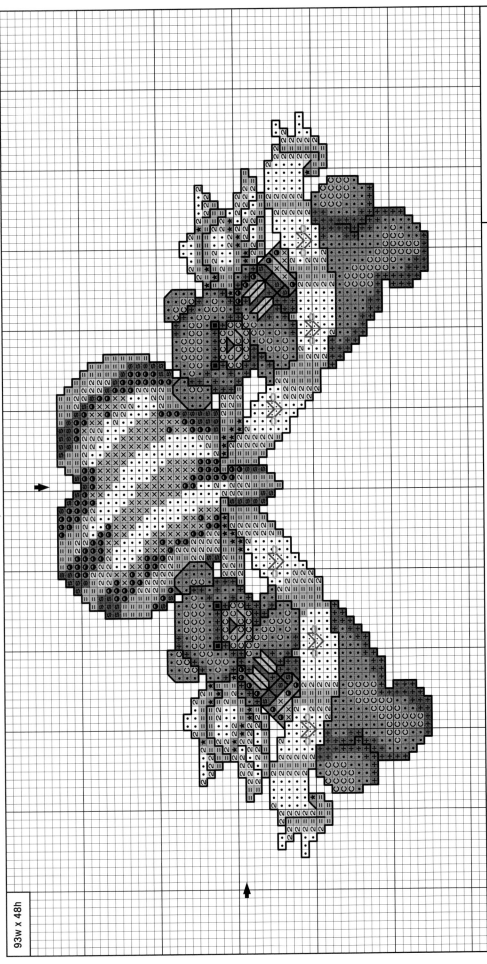

93w x 48h

The design was stitched over a 15" x 10" piece of 8.5 mesh waste canvas on a sweater. Six strands of floss were used for Cross Stitch and 2 strands for Backstitch and Lazy Daisy Stitches.

Working on Waste Canvas: Waste canvas is a special canvas that provides an evenweave grid for placing stitches on fabric. After the design is worked over the canvas, the canvas threads are removed, leaving the design on the fabric. The canvas is available in several mesh sizes.

Step 1. Cut waste canvas 2" larger than design on all sides. Cut interfacing same size as canvas. Cover edges of canvas with masking tape.

Step 2. Find desired placement for design; mark center of design on sweater with a pin.

Step 3. Match center of canvas to pin. Use the blue threads in canvas to place canvas straight on sweater; pin canvas to sweater. Pin interfacing to wrong side of sweater. Baste canvas to sweater through all three layers.

Step 4. Place sweater in a screw-type hoop. We recommend a hoop that is large enough to encircle entire design.

Step 5. Work design, stitching from large holes to large holes.

Step 6. Trim canvas to within ¾" of design. Dampen canvas until it becomes limp. Using tweezers, pull out canvas threads one at a time.

Design by Vicky Howard.

Marching to the rhythm of horn and drum, these parading bears capture the heartbeat of our great nation — and show that patriotism is a family affair!

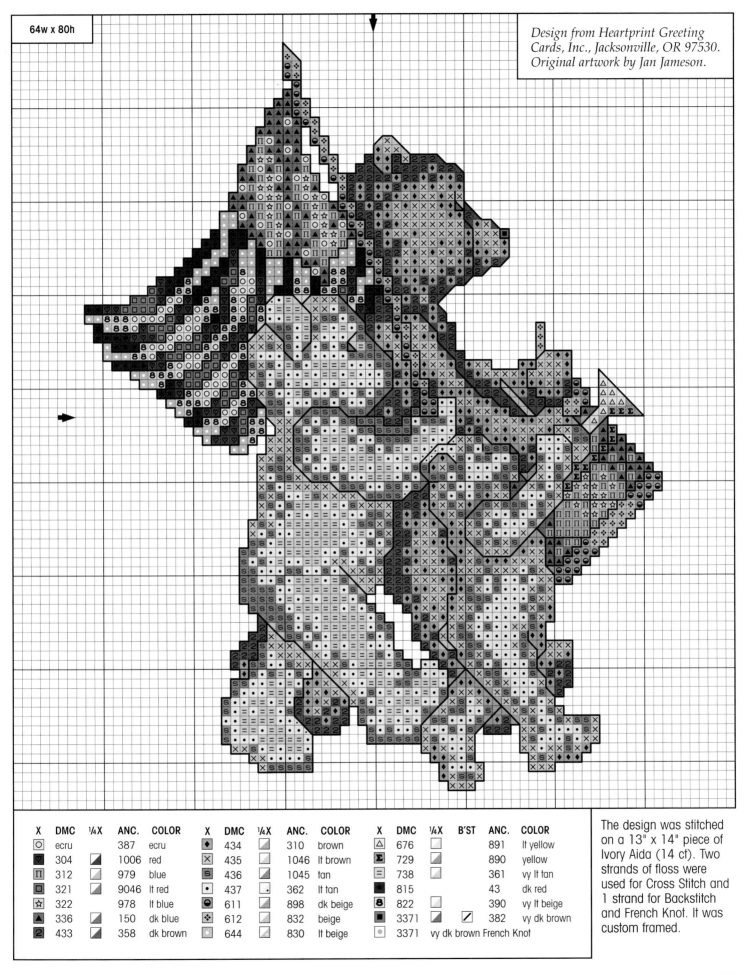

64w x 80h

Design from Heartprint Greeting Cards, Inc., Jacksonville, OR 97530. Original artwork by Jan Jameson.

X	DMC	¼X	ANC.	COLOR	X	DMC	¼X	ANC.	COLOR	X	DMC	¼X	B'ST	ANC.	COLOR
O	ecru		387	ecru	◆	434		310	brown	△	676			891	lt yellow
♥	304		1006	red	X	435		1046	lt brown	Σ	729			890	yellow
Π	312		979	blue	S	436		1045	tan	=	738			361	vy lt tan
▢	321		9046	lt red	•	437		362	lt tan	✱	815			43	dk red
☆	322		978	lt blue	◕	611		898	dk beige	8	822			390	vy lt beige
▲	336		150	dk blue	✤	612		832	beige	▪	3371			382	vy dk brown
2	433		358	dk brown	▫	644		830	lt beige	●	3371				vy dk brown French Knot

The design was stitched on a 13" x 14" piece of Ivory Aida (14 ct). Two strands of floss were used for Cross Stitch and 1 strand for Backstitch and French Knot. It was custom framed.

89

You'll be ready for Halloween dressed in this "beary" spooky sweatshirt featuring a witch and her creepy-crawly friend.

X	DMC	¼X	B'ST	ANC.	COLOR
■	310	◪	◪	403	black
◨	317	◪		400	grey
⊠	318	◪		399	lt grey
◼	321	◪		9046	red
∨	413	◪		401	dk grey
◕	433	◪		358	dk brown
★	434	◪		310	brown
•	435	◪		1046	lt brown
△	436	◪		1045	dk tan
☆	437			362	tan
◪	550	◪		102	dk purple
◨	552	◪		99	purple
◎	553	◪		98	lt purple
□	554	◪		96	vy lt purple
✳	666			46	lt red
–	738			361	lt tan
◆	780	◪		310	dk gold
◐	782	◪		308	gold
+	783	□		307	lt gold
✺	3799	◪		236	vy dk grey
●	310				black French Knot

44w x 87h

The **entire design** was stitched over a 9" x 14" piece of 8.5 mesh waste canvas on a sweatshirt. The **spider only** was stitched over a 3½" square of 8.5 mesh waste canvas on a turtleneck shirt. Six strands of floss were used for Cross Stitch and 2 strands for Backstitch and French Knots. See Working on Waste Canvas, page 143.

Design by Kathie Rueger. Needlework adaptation by Mike Vickery.

A thankful Pilgrim couple highlights our wall hanging for Thanksgiving, a time for families to rejoice in America's bounty.

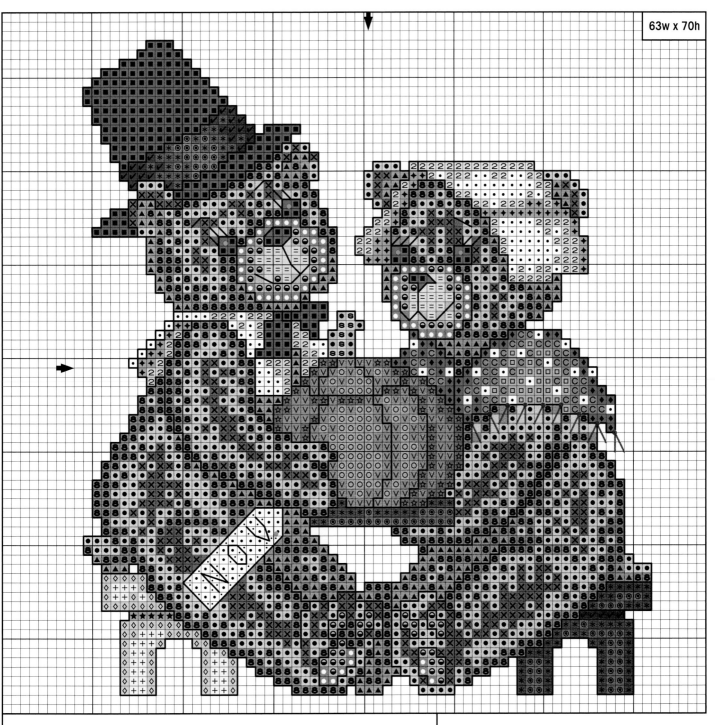

X	DMC	¼X	B'ST	ANC.	COLOR	X	DMC	¼X	B'ST	ANC.	COLOR
•	blanc	▨		2	white	◯	722			323	lt orange
✔	304			1006	dk red	◇	725			305	dk yellow
■	310	◩	◢	403	black	✛	726			295	yellow
◆	312		◢	979	dk blue	◓	738			361	lt tan
✳	321			9046	red	═	739	▢		387	vy lt tan
C	322			978	blue	★	783			307	gold
❽	433	◪		358	lt brown	▲	801			359	brown
●	434	◪		310	vy lt brown	⦿	911			205	green
✕	435	◪		1046	dk tan	S	912			209	lt green
◯	437	◪		362	tan	2	3072			847	vy lt grey
✦	648			900	lt grey	▢	3755			140	lt blue
◉	666			46	lt red	◦	blanc				white French Knot
✪	720			326	dk orange	◉	310				black French Knot
V	721			324	orange	●	312				dk blue French Knot

The design was stitched over 2 fabric threads on a 15" x 16" piece of Ivory Aida (18 ct). Six strands of floss were used for Cross Stitch and 2 strands for Backstitch and French Knots. It was made into a wall hanging. See Wall Hanging Finishing, page 144.

Design by Delane Lange.

Surprise someone you love with an early Christmas gift! One of these festive sweatshirts will spread holiday cheer all season long.

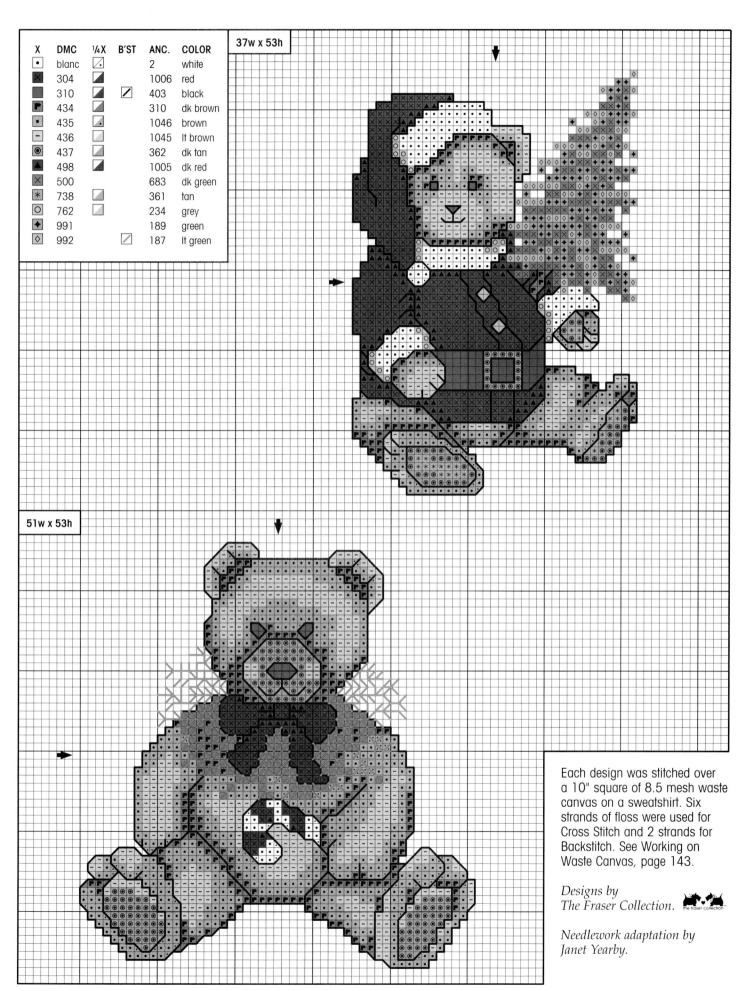

X	DMC	¼X	B'ST	ANC.	COLOR
•	blanc			2	white
✕	304			1006	red
	310		╱	403	black
�P	434			310	dk brown
•	435			1046	brown
−	436			1045	lt brown
⊙	437			362	dk tan
▲	498			1005	dk red
✕	500			683	dk green
✳	738			361	tan
○	762			234	grey
✦	991			189	green
◇	992		╱	187	lt green

37w x 53h

51w x 53h

Each design was stitched over a 10" square of 8.5 mesh waste canvas on a sweatshirt. Six strands of floss were used for Cross Stitch and 2 strands for Backstitch. See Working on Waste Canvas, page 143.

Designs by
The Fraser Collection.

the fraser collection

Needlework adaptation by
Janet Yearby.

Sending Christmas cards, wrapping gifts, and baking goodies are all activities that keep us busy at Christmastime. This whimsical set of ornaments captures these memorable moments with charm.

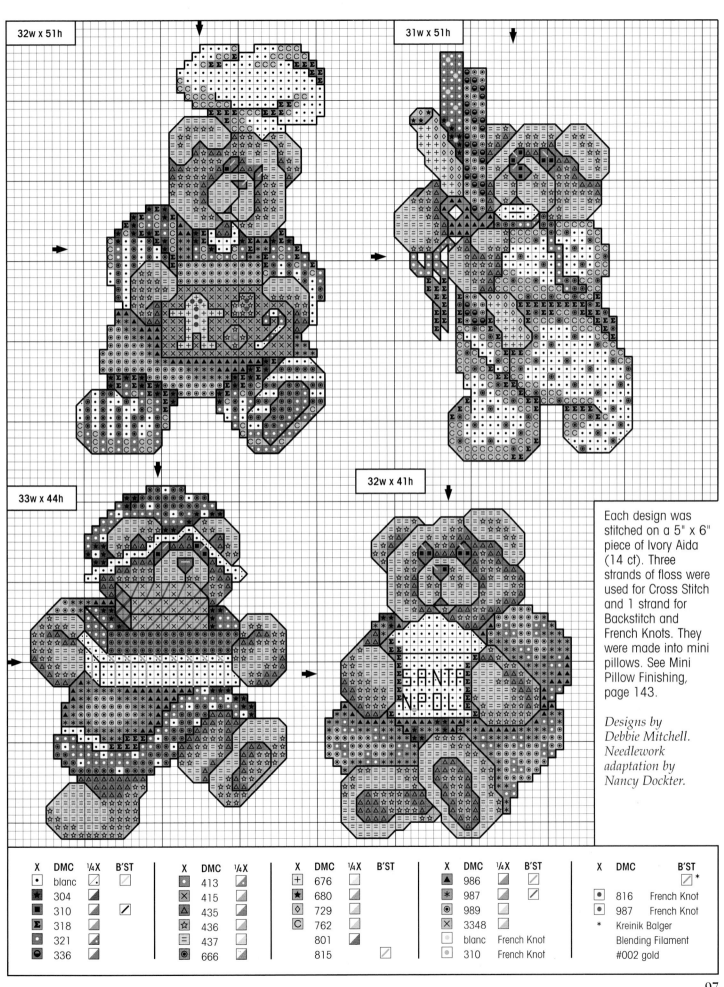

Each design was stitched on a 5" x 6" piece of Ivory Aida (14 ct). Three strands of floss were used for Cross Stitch and 1 strand for Backstitch and French Knots. They were made into mini pillows. See Mini Pillow Finishing, page 143.

Designs by Debbie Mitchell. Needlework adaptation by Nancy Dockter.

X	DMC	1/4X	B'ST
•	blanc		
★	304		
■	310		
Σ	318		
•	321		
◐	336		

X	DMC	1/4X
•	413	
X	415	
△	435	
☆	436	
=	437	
◉	666	

X	DMC	1/4X	B'ST
+	676		
★	680		
◇	729		
C	762		
	801		
	815		

X	DMC	1/4X	B'ST
▲	986		
✳	987		
◉	989		
X	3348		
	blanc	French Knot	
	310	French Knot	

X	DMC	B'ST
		*
⊙	816	French Knot
•	987	French Knot
*	Kreinik Balger	
	Blending Filament	
	#002 gold	

Very Vogue Teddies

Teddy bears have been in vogue since they were first introduced in the early 1900's. To celebrate the enduring popularity of the cuddly toy, we've created a whole collection of wonderful wearables. You'll find adorable items for grownups as well as youngsters and babies. The humorous sentiment on this "Beary" Cute Shirt *makes it a great choice for wearing on your birthday. These embellished fashions will capture your heart!*

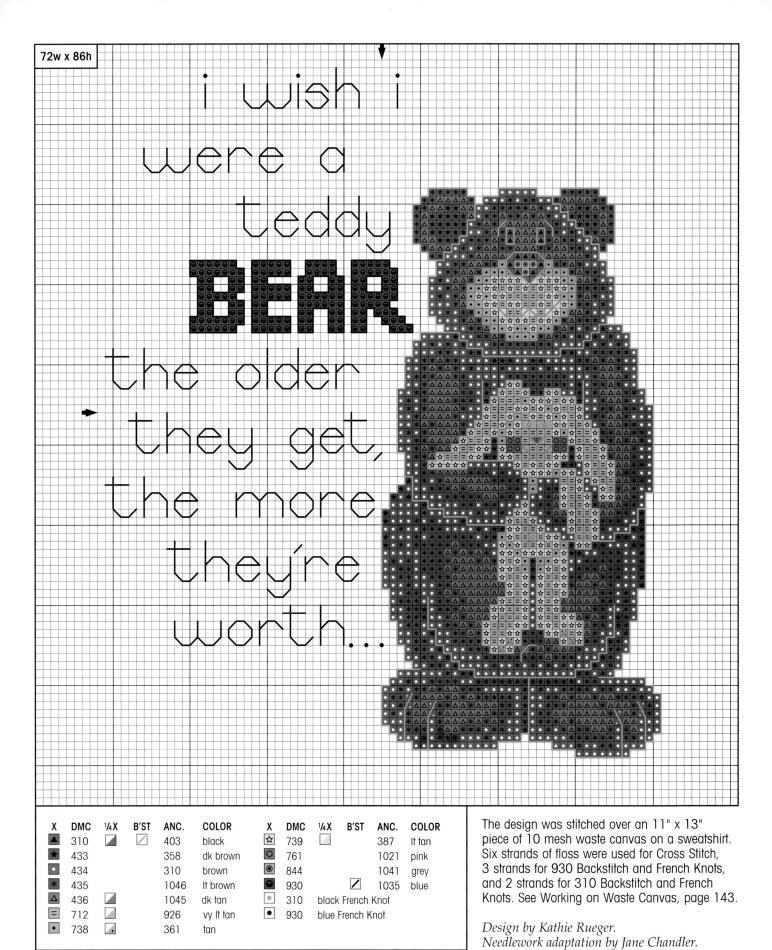

i wish i
were a
teddy
BEAR
the older
they get,
the more
they're
worth...

72w x 86h

X	DMC	¼X	B'ST	ANC.	COLOR
▲	310	◢	◿	403	black
★	433			358	dk brown
•	434			310	brown
*	435			1046	lt brown
△	436	◢		1045	dk tan
=	712	◢		926	vy lt tan
•	738	◢		361	tan

X	DMC	¼X	B'ST	ANC.	COLOR
☆	739	◢		387	lt tan
○	761			1021	pink
◉	844			1041	grey
◕	930		◿	1035	blue
•	310				black French Knot
•	930				blue French Knot

The design was stitched over an 11" x 13" piece of 10 mesh waste canvas on a sweatshirt. Six strands of floss were used for Cross Stitch, 3 strands for 930 Backstitch and French Knots, and 2 strands for 310 Backstitch and French Knots. See Working on Waste Canvas, page 143.

Design by Kathie Rueger.
Needlework adaptation by Jane Chandler.

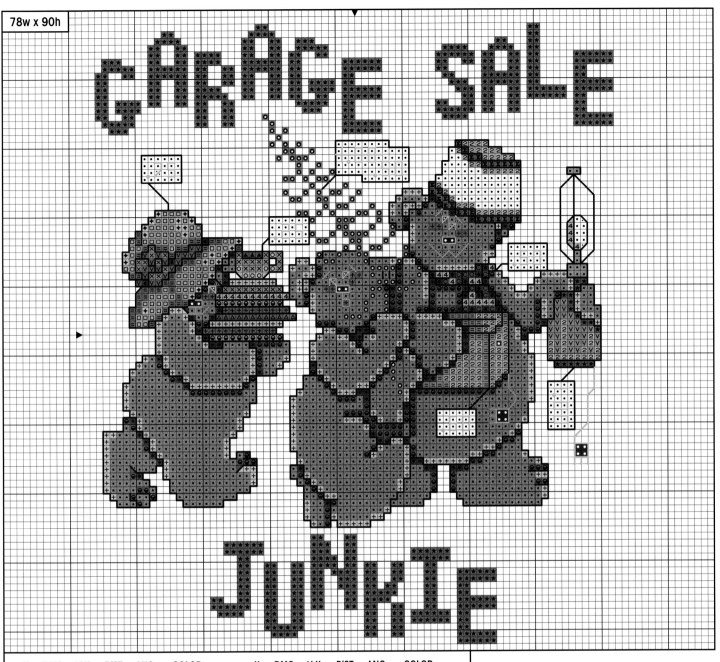

78w x 90h

The design was stitched over a 14" x 15" piece of 8.5 mesh waste canvas on a sweatshirt. Six strands of floss were used for Cross Stitch and 2 strands for Backstitch and French Knots, unless otherwise noted in color key. See Working on Waste Canvas, page 143.

Design by Karen Wood.

Cloaked in a kaleidoscope of brightly colored leaves, this free-spirited bear enjoys a playful autumn afternoon. To enhance the design, we stitched it on a forest green sweatshirt.

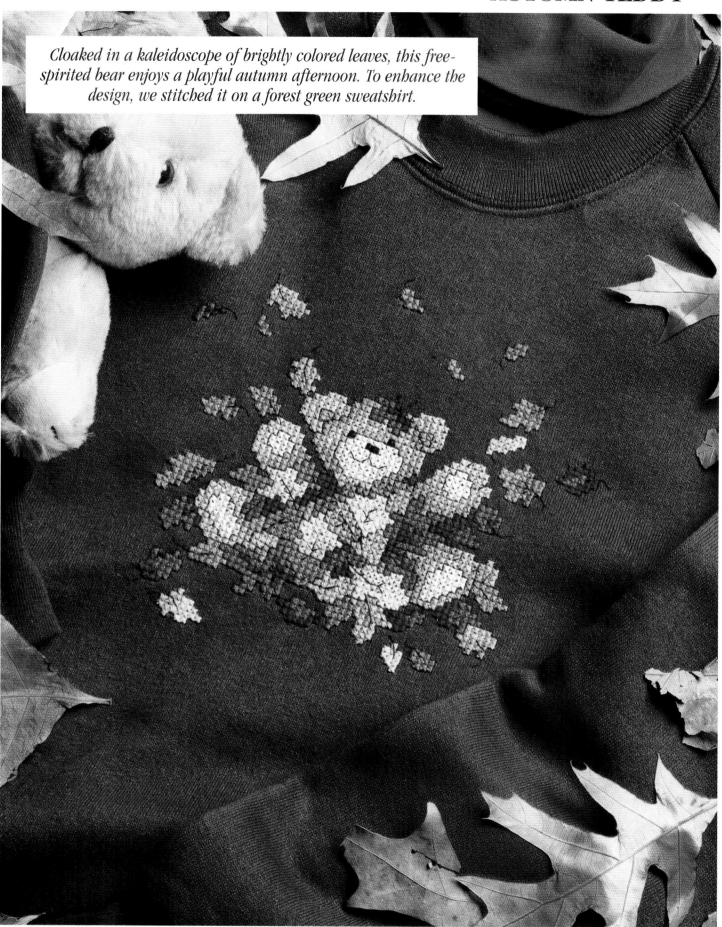

106

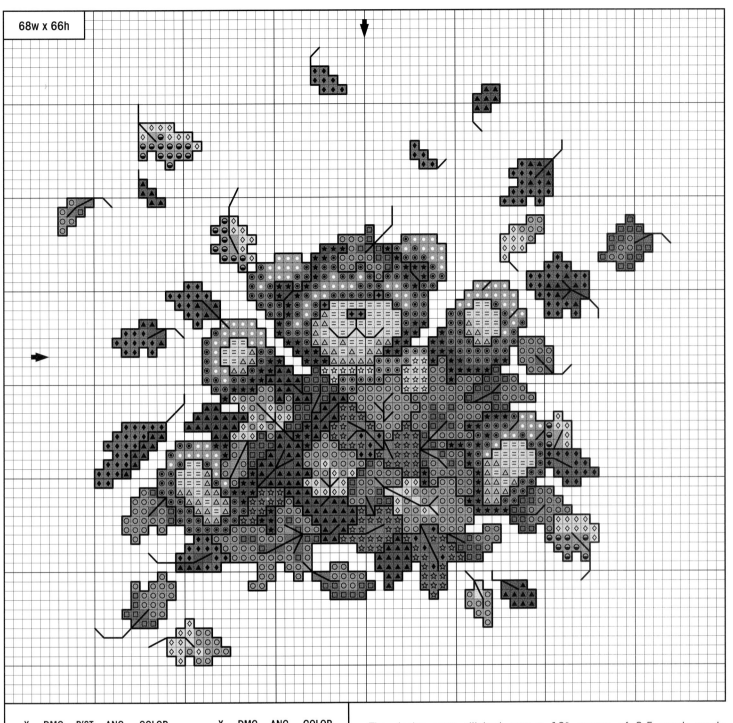

68w x 66h

X	DMC	B'ST	ANC.	COLOR		X	DMC	ANC.	COLOR
✦	310	╱	403	black		◐	725	305	yellow
◎	350		11	lt red		△	738	361	tan
★	435		1046	dk brown		═	739	387	lt tan
◉	436		1045	brown		◓	782	308	gold
●	437		362	lt brown		◇	783	307	lt gold
▲	720		326	dk orange		☆	813	161	lt blue
◆	721		324	orange		▣	817	13	red
☆	722		323	lt orange		◉	826	161	blue

The design was stitched over a 12" square of 8.5 mesh waste canvas on a sweatshirt. Six strands of floss were used for Cross Stitch and 2 strands for Backstitch. See Working on Waste Canvas, page 143.

Design by Ginny Fraser.
Needlework adaptation by Kathy Elrod.

Faced with an assortment of tempting goodies that are too delicious to resist, this teddy issues a chocolate-lover's plea. The winsome design is stitched on an apron to please a cook.

Deliver me from evil but leave my chocolate alone!

X	DMC	¼X	B'ST	ANC.	COLOR
•	blanc			2	white
■	318			399	dk grey
■	321	◪	◪	9046	red
Σ	335			38	dk pink
▣	415			398	grey
✦	433	◪		358	lt brown
▲	434			310	vy lt brown
▣	435			1046	vy dk tan
✚	436	◪		1045	dk tan
S	437	◪		362	tan
◉	666	◪		46	lt red
2	738			361	lt tan
✳	739			387	vy lt tan
O	762			234	lt grey
V	801		◪	359	brown
★	839			360	dk beige brown
△	840			379	beige brown
❖	841			378	lt beige brown
☆	899			52	pink
■	938			381	dk brown
◇	3326			36	lt pink
◨	3371	◪	◪	382	vy dk brown

The design was stitched over a 16" x 12" piece of 8.5 mesh waste canvas on the bib of an apron. Six strands of floss were used for Cross Stitch, 3 strands for red Backstitch and brown Backstitch, and 2 strands for all other Backstitch.

Working on Waste Canvas: Waste canvas is a special canvas that provides an evenweave grid for placing stitches on fabric. After the design is worked over the canvas, the canvas threads are removed, leaving the design on the fabric. The canvas is available in several mesh sizes.

Step 1. Cover edges of canvas with masking tape.

Step 2. Find desired placement for design; mark center of design on apron with a pin.

Step 3. Match center of canvas to pin. Use the blue threads in canvas to place canvas straight on apron; pin canvas to apron. Baste canvas to apron.

Step 4. Place apron in a screw-type hoop. We recommend a hoop that is large enough to encircle entire design.

Step 5. Using a sharp needle, work design, stitching from large holes to large holes.

Step 6. Trim canvas to within ¾" of design. Dampen canvas until it becomes limp. Using tweezers, pull out canvas threads one at a time.

Design by Debra Jordan Meyer.

Embellishing a T-shirt, this "beary" cute ladybug is bound to bring lots of luck. A familiar children's rhyme enhances the summery design.

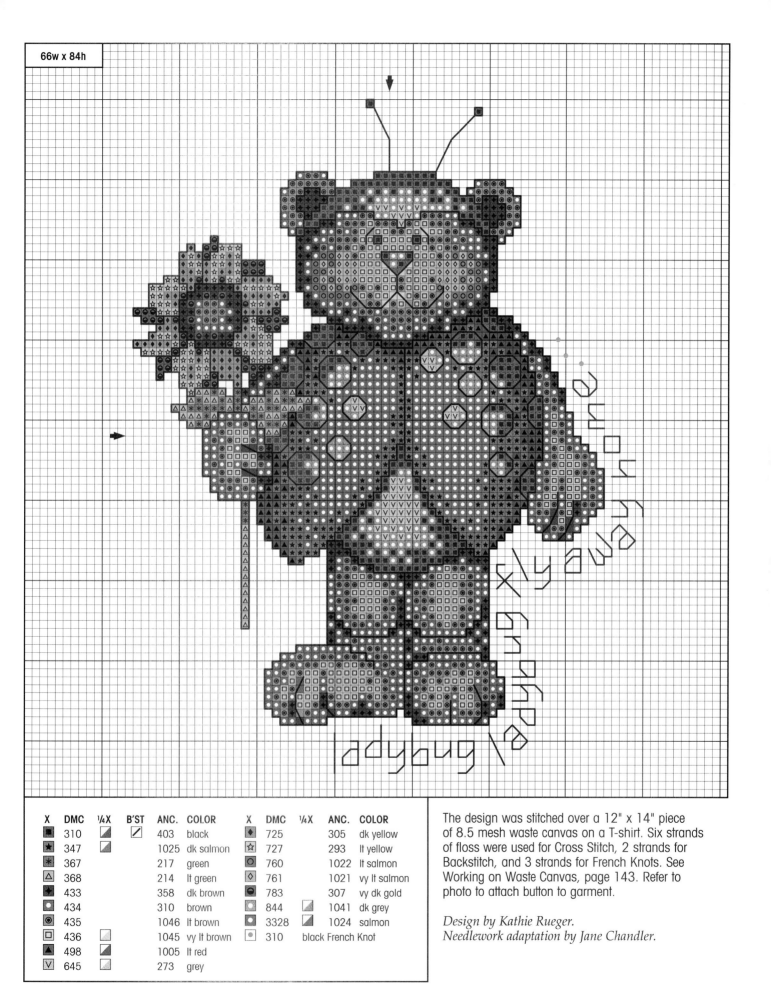

66w x 84h

X	DMC	¼X	B'ST	ANC.	COLOR	X	DMC	¼X	ANC.	COLOR
■	310	◢	◢	403	black	◆	725		305	dk yellow
★	347	◢		1025	dk salmon	☆	727		293	lt yellow
✱	367			217	green	◎	760		1022	lt salmon
△	368			214	lt green	◇	761		1021	vy lt salmon
✦	433			358	dk brown	◓	783		307	vy dk gold
◉	434			310	brown	◨	844	◢	1041	dk grey
◉	435			1046	lt brown	◉	3328	◢	1024	salmon
□	436	◢		1045	vy lt brown	●	310			black French Knot
▲	498			1005	lt red					
V	645	◢		273	grey					

The design was stitched over a 12" x 14" piece of 8.5 mesh waste canvas on a T-shirt. Six strands of floss were used for Cross Stitch, 2 strands for Backstitch, and 3 strands for French Knots. See Working on Waste Canvas, page 143. Refer to photo to attach button to garment.

Design by Kathie Rueger.
Needlework adaptation by Jane Chandler.

Like flowers in a bouquet, when loved ones are gathered together they create something beautiful. This little country teddy bear and her feathered friends pass on this lesson of the heart.

GIVE LOVE

GATHER LOVE

59w x 79h

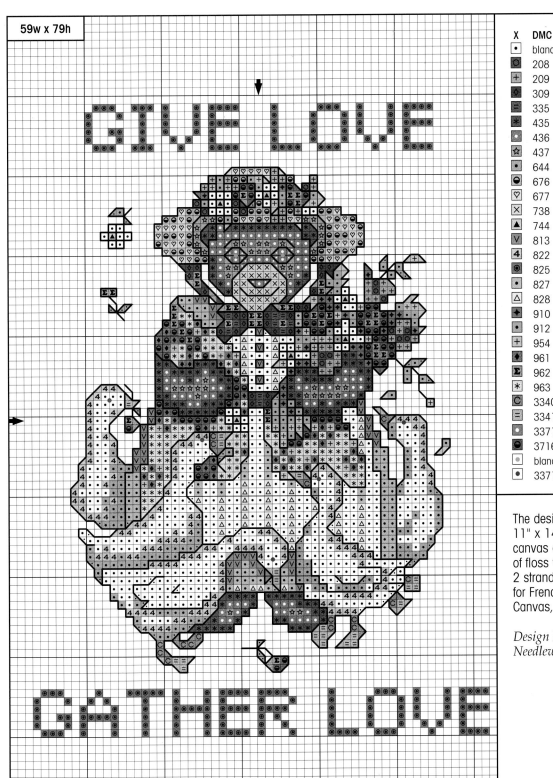

X	DMC	¼X	B'ST	ANC.	COLOR
•	blanc			2	white
◎	208			110	purple
+	209			109	lt purple
◈	309			42	dk rose
▦	335			38	vy dk pink
✳	435			1046	dk brown
◉	436			1045	brown
☆	437			362	lt brown
•	644			830	beige
◖	676			891	tan
♡	677			886	lt tan
✕	738			361	vy lt brown
▲	744			301	yellow
V	813			161	blue
4	822			390	lt beige
◎	825			162	dk blue
•	827			160	lt blue
△	828			9159	vy lt blue
✦	910			229	dk green
✦	912			209	green
+	954			203	lt green
◆	961			76	dk pink
Σ	962			75	pink
✳	963			73	vy lt pink
C	3340			329	orange
=	3341			328	lt orange
◉	3371		/	382	brown black
◐	3716			25	lt pink
◦	blanc				white French Knot
•	3371				brown black French Knot

The design was stitched over an 11" x 14" piece of 8.5 mesh waste canvas on a sweatshirt. Six strands of floss were used for Cross Stitch, 2 strands for Backstitch, and 4 strands for French Knots. See Working on Waste Canvas, page 143.

Design by Kim Stenbo for Figi Graphics.
Needlework adaptation by Mike Vickery.

Any nurse will love this sweatshirt! Nurse Bear ministers to a tearful little patient in our tongue-in-cheek design.

X	DMC	¼X	B'ST	ANC.	COLOR
•	blanc			2	white
■	304			1006	dk red
■	310	◩	◹	403	black
★	318			399	dk grey
⬣	321		◹	9046	red
≡	415	◩		398	grey
◉	433	◪		358	vy dk brown
C	434	◪		310	dk brown
✕	435	◪		1046	brown
+	436	◩		1045	lt brown
○	738	◩		361	vy lt brown
⊙	310	black French Knot			
⊘	827	blue Lazy Daisy Stitch			

The design was stitched over a 12" x 10" piece of 8.5 mesh waste canvas on a sweatshirt. Six strands of floss were used for Cross Stitch and 2 strands for Backstitch, French Knots, and Lazy Daisy Stitches. See Working on Waste Canvas, page 143.

Design by Kathie Rueger.

67w x 48h

CAMPFIRE BEARS

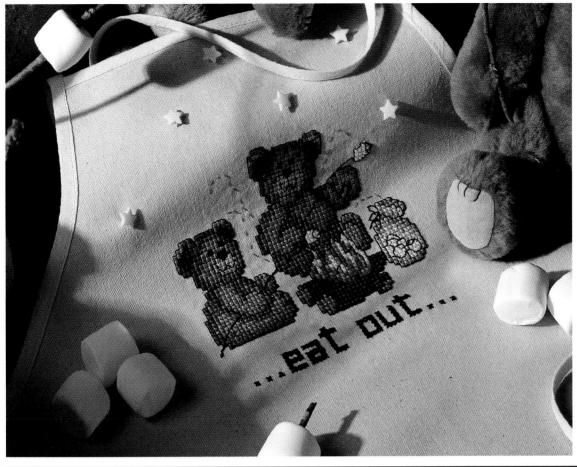

Who can resist the fun of "eating out" in the great outdoors? Certainly not these bears! Stitched on a canvas apron, our campfire design is just the thing for a summertime cookout.

56w x 51h

X	DMC	1/4X	B'ST	ANC.	COLOR
•	blanc			2	white
○	307			289	yellow
▓	310		╱	403	black
C	318			399	grey
	414		╱	235	dk grey
◉	415			398	lt grey
●	434			310	vy dk tan
X	435			1046	dk tan
S	436			1045	tan
✤	437			362	lt tan
+	738			361	vy lt tan
□	740		╱	316	orange
Σ	762			234	vy lt grey
⊟	801			359	brown
▣	898		╱	360	dk brown
V	946			332	dk orange
●	310	black French Knot			

The design was stitched over an 11" x 10" piece of 8.5 mesh waste canvas on the bib of an apron. Six strands of floss were used for Cross Stitch, 4 strands for dk brown Backstitch, and 2 strands for all other Backstitch and French Knots. See Working on Waste Canvas, page 143. Refer to photo for placement of star buttons.

Design by Kathie Rueger.

For The Fun Of It

Laughter is good for the soul, as the teddy bears in this collection all know! Portraying events from everyday life, these fun-filled designs invite you to smile, be happy, and make gloomy days sunny. Anyone who's ever faced a mountain of laundry will appreciate Another Day in Paradise, *which makes light of housework. You'll find other humorous observations about life as you turn the pages, along with poignant images of memorable moments such as a child's first haircut.*

day "... paradise...

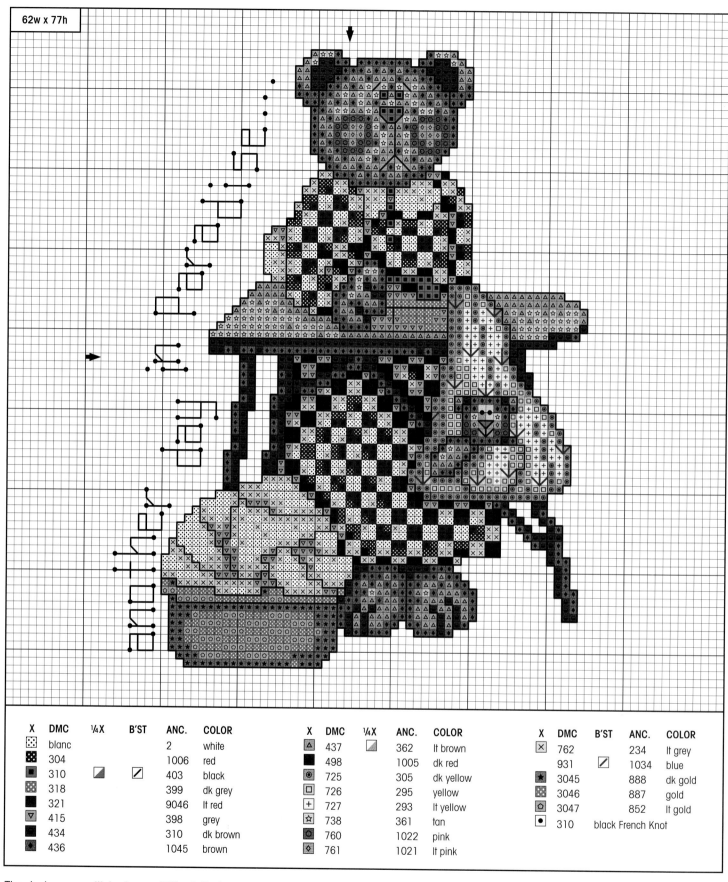

X	DMC	¼X	B'ST	ANC.	COLOR		X	DMC	¼X	ANC.	COLOR		X	DMC	B'ST	ANC.	COLOR
	blanc			2	white		▲	437	◩	362	lt brown		✕	762		234	lt grey
✶	304			1006	red		■	498		1005	dk red			931	◩	1034	blue
▪	310	◩	◩	403	black		◉	725		305	dk yellow		★	3045		888	dk gold
▨	318			399	dk grey		▢	726		295	yellow		▨	3046		887	gold
◼	321			9046	lt red		+	727		293	lt yellow		⬠	3047		852	lt gold
▽	415			398	grey		☆	738		361	tan		●	310			black French Knot
◼	434			310	dk brown		◎	760		1022	pink						
◆	436			1045	brown		◇	761		1021	lt pink						

The design was stitched on a 13" x 14" piece of Ivory Aida (14 ct). Three strands of floss were used for Cross Stitch and 1 strand for Backstitch and French Knots. It was custom framed.

Design by Kathie Rueger. Needlework adaptation by Cara Gist.

Any time you're feeling "frazzled," our sweet teddy bear mug will make you smile. The cheery project will also make a fun gift for a busy friend.

X	DMC	B'ST	ANC.	COLOR	X	DMC	ANC.	COLOR
Π	310	✓	403	black	=	738	361	tan
▼	433		358	dk brown	☆	739	387	lt tan
◈	435		1046	brown	✚	930	1035	dk blue
✕	436		1045	lt brown	❖	932	1033	blue
O	676		891	gold	◉	938	381	vy dk brown
>	677		886	lt gold	✿	3829		vy dk gold
♥	729		890	dk gold	•	310		black French Knot

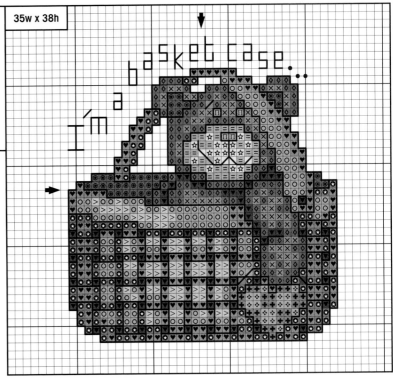

35w x 38h

The design was stitched on a 10¼" x 3½" piece of Vinyl-Weave™ (14 ct). Three strands of floss were used for Cross Stitch and 1 strand for Backstitch and French Knots. It was inserted in a beige mug.

For design placement, fold vinyl in half, matching short edges. Center design on right half of vinyl if mug is to be used by a right-handed person or on the left half if mug is to be used by a left-handed person. Hand wash mug to protect stitchery.

Design by Kathie Rueger.
Needlework adaptation by Jane Chandler.

A nice long bubble bath is a luxurious way to escape the frustrations of the day! This nostalgic bear will help you get the message across when you need a little quiet time.

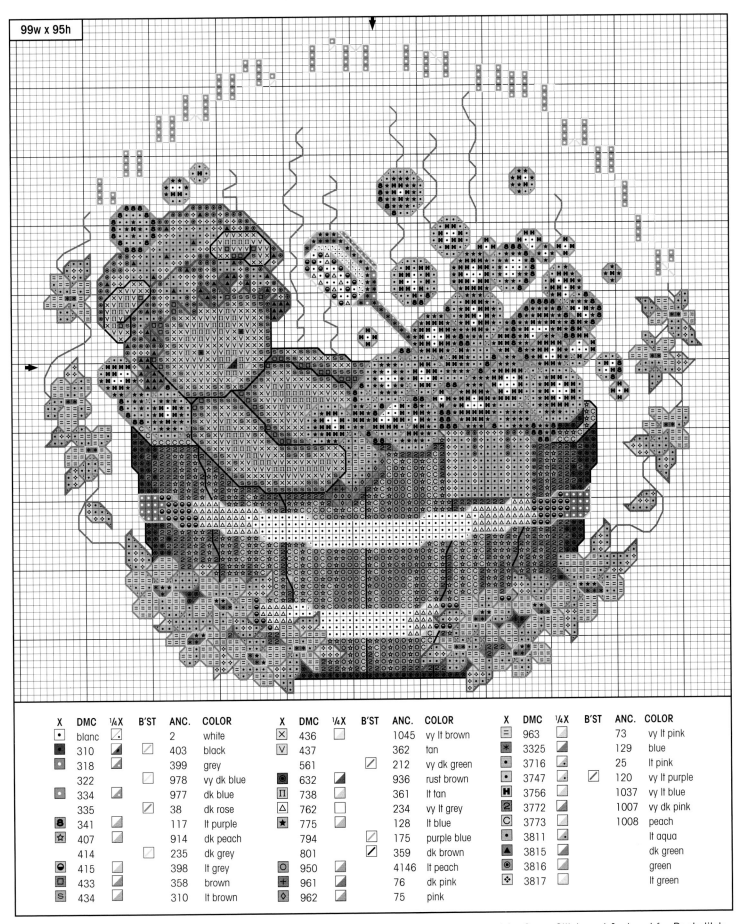

99w x 95h

X	DMC	¼X	B'ST	ANC.	COLOR	X	DMC	¼X	B'ST	ANC.	COLOR	X	DMC	¼X	B'ST	ANC.	COLOR
•	blanc			2	white	✕	436			1045	vy lt brown	=	963			73	vy lt pink
●	310		✓	403	black	V	437			362	tan	✱	3325			129	blue
◎	318			399	grey		561		✓	212	vy dk green	•	3716			25	lt pink
	322			978	vy dk blue	◉	632			936	rust brown	•	3747			120	vy lt purple
◉	334			977	dk blue	Π	738			361	lt tan	H	3756			1037	vy lt blue
	335		✓	38	dk rose	△	762			234	vy lt grey	2	3772			1007	vy dk pink
8	341			117	lt purple	★	775			128	lt blue	C	3773			1008	peach
☆	407			914	dk peach		794		✓	175	purple blue	•	3811				lt aqua
	414			235	dk grey		801		✓	359	dk brown	▲	3815				dk green
◉	415			398	lt grey	◎	950			4146	lt peach	◉	3816				green
◻	433			358	brown	✚	961			76	dk pink	❖	3817				lt green
S	434			310	lt brown	◇	962			75	pink						

The design was stitched on a 10" square of Ivory Aida (18 ct). Two strands of floss were used for Cross Stitch and 1 strand for Backstitch. It was inserted in a purchased towel bar frame (6¼" dia. opening).

Design by Debra Jordan Bryan. Needlework adaptation by Jane Chandler.

This adorably grumpy teddy commemorates one of life's little milestones — a child's first haircut. The design can be custom framed for a sweet addition to a child's room or a friend's bear collection, or you can personalize it for an unforgettable keepsake.

FIRST HAIRCUT

Chelsea 1-8-96

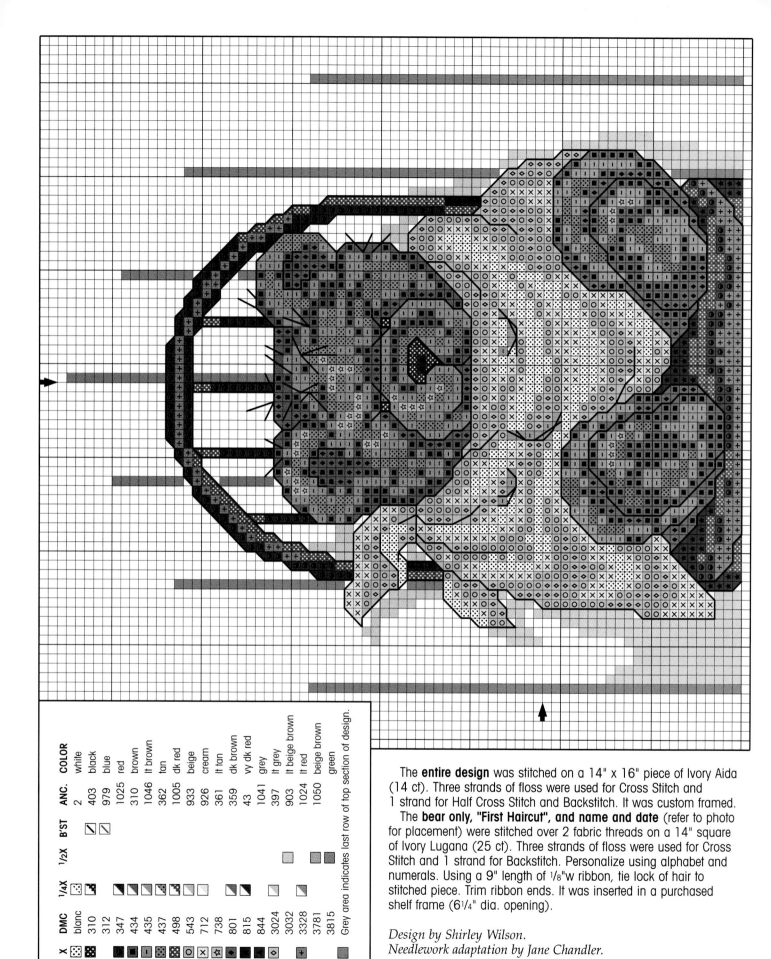

X	DMC	1/4X	1/2X	B'ST	ANC.	COLOR
	blanc				2	white
	310				403	black
	312				979	blue
	347				1025	red
	434				310	brown
	435				1046	lt brown
	437				362	tan
	498				1005	dk red
	543				933	beige
	712				926	cream
	738				361	lt tan
	801				359	dk brown
	815				43	vy dk red
	844				1041	grey
	3024				397	lt grey
	3032				903	lt beige brown
	3328				1024	lt red
	3781				1050	beige brown
	3815					green

Grey area indicates last row of top section of design.

The **entire design** was stitched on a 14" x 16" piece of Ivory Aida (14 ct). Three strands of floss were used for Cross Stitch and 1 strand for Half Cross Stitch and Backstitch. It was custom framed.

The **bear only, "First Haircut", and name and date** (refer to photo for placement) were stitched over 2 fabric threads on a 14" square of Ivory Lugana (25 ct). Three strands of floss were used for Cross Stitch and 1 strand for Backstitch. Personalize using alphabet and numerals. Using a 9" length of 1/8"w ribbon, tie lock of hair to stitched piece. Trim ribbon ends. It was inserted in a purchased shelf frame (6 1/4" dia. opening).

Design by Shirley Wilson.
Needlework adaptation by Jane Chandler.

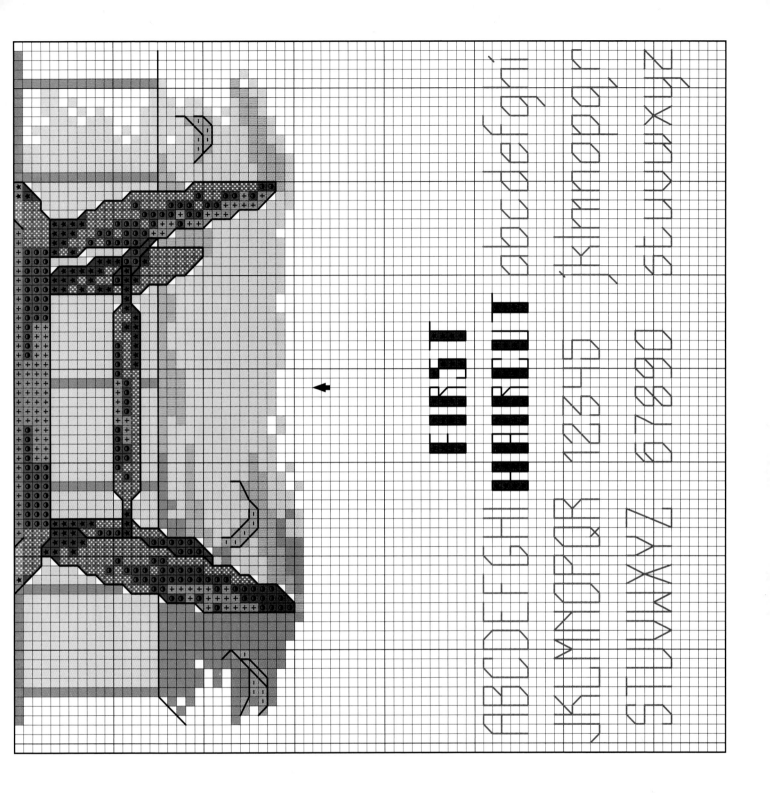

abcdefghi
jklmnopqr
stuvwxyz
0123456789

ABCDEFGHI
JKLMNOPQR
STUVWXYZ
1234567890

FIRST
MIDDLE

Fast and efficient, the microwave oven gives busy cooks more leisure time to enjoy family, friends, and of course, cross stitching!

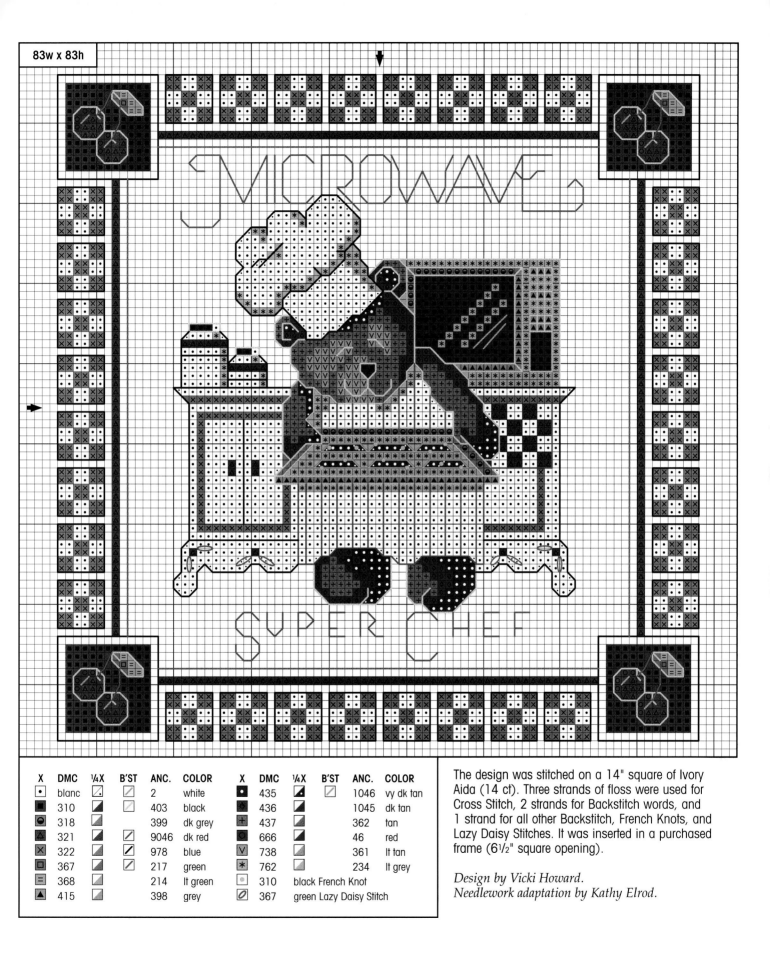

83w x 83h

X	DMC	¼X	B'ST	ANC.	COLOR	X	DMC	¼X	B'ST	ANC.	COLOR
•	blanc			2	white	◐	435			1046	vy dk tan
■	310			403	black	■	436			1045	dk tan
◉	318			399	dk grey	+	437			362	tan
▲	321			9046	dk red	◉	666			46	red
✕	322			978	blue	V	738			361	lt tan
▣	367			217	green	*	762			234	lt grey
☰	368			214	lt green	•	310				black French Knot
▲	415			398	grey	∅	367				green Lazy Daisy Stitch

The design was stitched on a 14" square of Ivory Aida (14 ct). Three strands of floss were used for Cross Stitch, 2 strands for Backstitch words, and 1 strand for all other Backstitch, French Knots, and Lazy Daisy Stitches. It was inserted in a purchased frame (6½" square opening).

Design by Vicki Howard.
Needlework adaptation by Kathy Elrod.

Grandma's fresh, home-baked cookies are every child's dream! This pot holder and mug are just the thing for snack time.

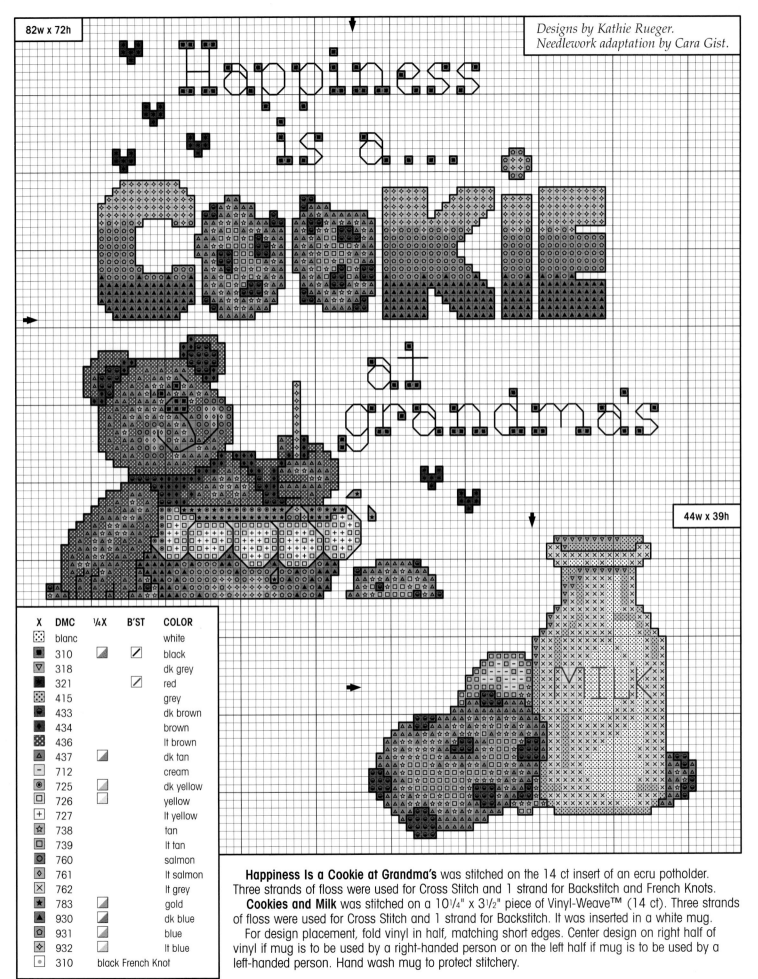

82w x 72h

Designs by Kathie Rueger.
Needlework adaptation by Cara Gist.

44w x 39h

X	DMC	¼X	B'ST	COLOR
	blanc			white
	310			black
	318			dk grey
	321			red
	415			grey
	433			dk brown
	434			brown
	436			lt brown
	437			dk tan
	712			cream
	725			dk yellow
	726			yellow
	727			lt yellow
	738			tan
	739			lt tan
	760			salmon
	761			lt salmon
	762			lt grey
	783			gold
	930			dk blue
	931			blue
	932			lt blue
	310			black French Knot

Happiness Is a Cookie at Grandma's was stitched on the 14 ct insert of an ecru potholder. Three strands of floss were used for Cross Stitch and 1 strand for Backstitch and French Knots.

Cookies and Milk was stitched on a 10¼" x 3½" piece of Vinyl-Weave™ (14 ct). Three strands of floss were used for Cross Stitch and 1 strand for Backstitch. It was inserted in a white mug. For design placement, fold vinyl in half, matching short edges. Center design on right half of vinyl if mug is to be used by a right-handed person or on the left half if mug is to be used by a left-handed person. Hand wash mug to protect stitchery.

Welcome a new neighbor or thank an old friend with a delicious treat from your kitchen. Tagged with our cute "flour power" chef, your gift is sure to express warm wishes.

X	DMC	¼X	B'ST	COLOR	X	DMC	¼X	B'ST	COLOR
•	blanc			white	✦	666			red
	310		✓	black	☆	739			lt tan
◐	434			dk tan	●	798		✓	blue
△	437			tan	=	809			lt blue
★	563			green	◆	898			brown
▣	632			mocha					

The design was stitched on a 7" square of White Aida (14 ct). Three strands of floss were used for Cross Stitch and 1 strand for Backstitch and French Knots. It was stiffened and made into a gift tag.

For stiffened tag, cut one piece of medium-weight cream fabric same size as stitched piece for backing. Apply a heavy coat of fabric stiffener to back of stitched piece using a small foam brush. Matching wrong sides, place stitched piece on backing fabric, smoothing stitched piece while pressing fabric pieces together; allow to dry. Apply fabric stiffener to backing fabric and allow to dry. Refer to photo to trim stitched piece. Using a hole punch, cut a hole at top of tag.

Design by Linda Gillum.

130

40w x 39h

A bucketful of bubbles makes bathtime more bearable for this endearing teddy. The lighthearted piece is ideal for the bathroom!

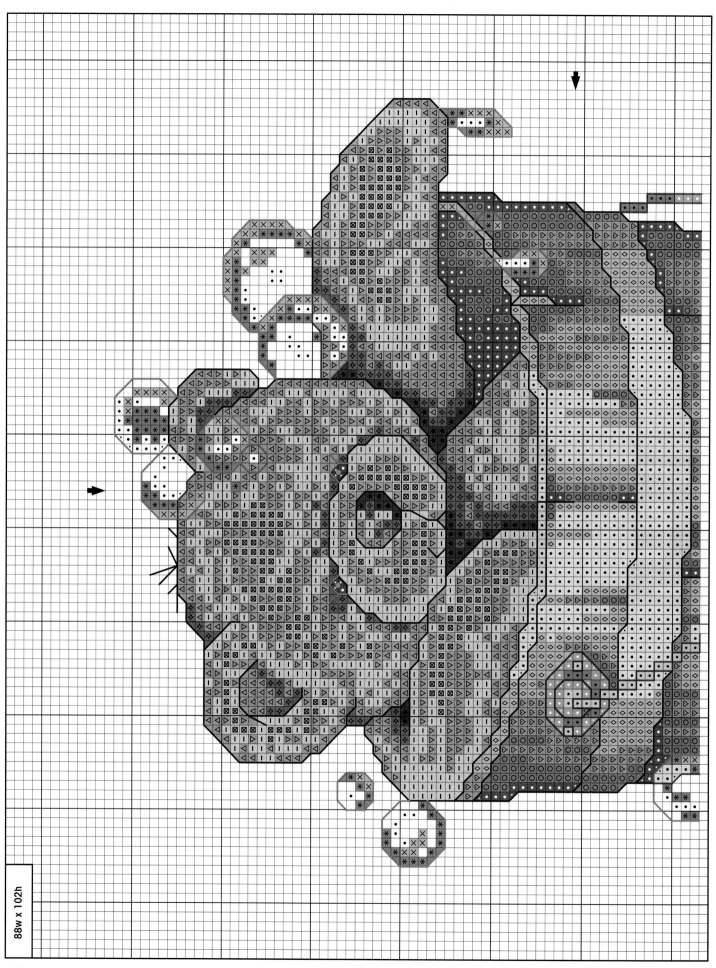

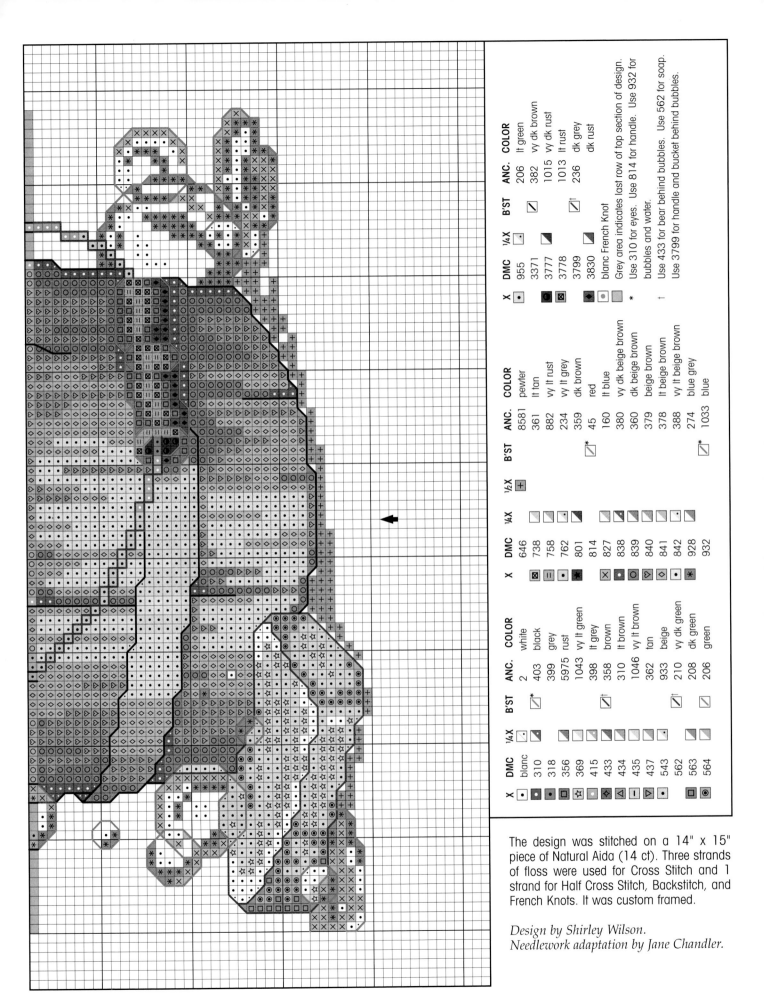

X	DMC	ANC.	COLOR
	955	206	lt green
	3371	382	vy dk brown
	3777	1015	vy dk rust
	3778	1013	lt rust
	3799	236	dk grey
	3830		dk rust
*	blanc		French Knot

Grey area indicates last row of top section of design. Use 310 for eyes. Use 814 for handle. Use 932 for bubbles and water. Use 433 for bear behind bubbles. Use 562 for soap. Use 3799 for handle and bucket behind bubbles.

X	DMC	ANC.	COLOR
	646	8581	pewter
	738	361	lt tan
	758	882	vy lt rust
	762	234	vy lt grey
	801	359	dk brown
	814	45	red
	827	160	lt blue
	838	380	vy dk beige brown
	839	360	dk beige brown
	840	379	beige brown
	841	378	lt beige brown
	842	388	vy lt beige brown
	928	274	blue grey
	932	1033	blue

X	DMC	ANC.	COLOR
	blanc	2	white
	310	403	black
	318	399	grey
	356	5975	rust
	369	1043	vy lt green
	415	398	lt grey
	433	358	brown
	434	310	lt brown
	435	1046	vy lt brown
	437	362	tan
	543	933	beige
	562	210	vy dk green
	563	208	dk green
	564	206	green

The design was stitched on a 14" x 15" piece of Natural Aida (14 ct). Three strands of floss were used for Cross Stitch and 1 strand for Half Cross Stitch, Backstitch, and French Knots. It was custom framed.

Design by Shirley Wilson.
Needlework adaptation by Jane Chandler.

Cuddlers young and old will find comfort in this cozy afghan — just like these two little cubs snuggled against their mama's soft shoulders. The touching trio will steal your heart away.

73w x 76h

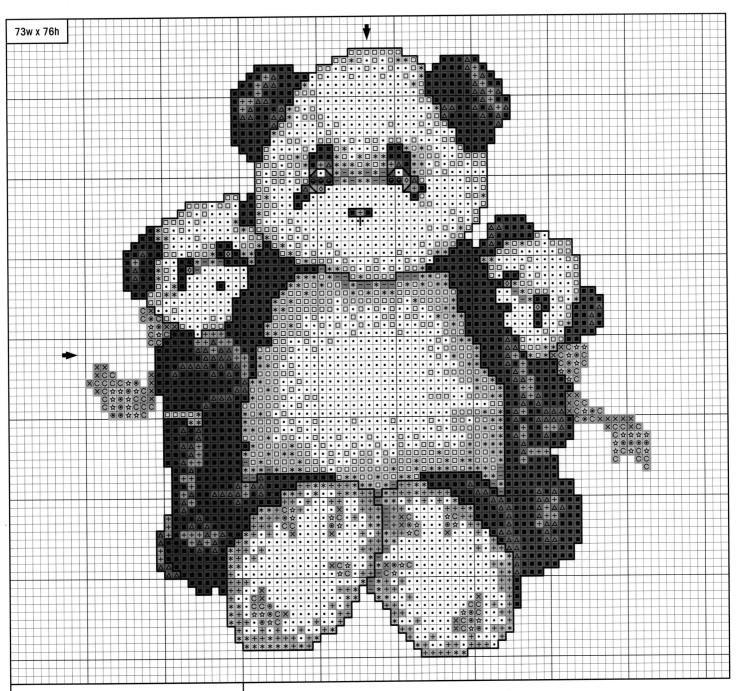

X	DMC	¼X	B'ST	ANC.	COLOR
•	blanc			2	white
■	310	◪	◪	403	black
+	317	◪		400	lt grey
	347		◪	1025	vy dk pink
◇	434	◪		310	lt brown
▨	642			392	dk tan
✳	644			830	tan
C	760			1022	pink
☆	761			1021	lt pink
◐	801	◪		359	brown
▢	822			390	lt tan
✕	3712			1023	dk pink
◉	3713			1020	vy lt pink
△	3799	◪		236	grey

The design was stitched over 2 fabric threads on a 45" x 58" piece (standard afghan size) of Antique Blue Anne Cloth (18 ct). Six strands of floss were used for Cross Stitch and 2 strands for Backstitch. Refer to Diagram for placement of design on fabric. It was made into an afghan.

For afghan, cut selvages from fabric; measure 5½" from raw edge of fabric and pull out one fabric thread. Fringe fabric up to missing thread. Repeat for each side. Tie an overhand knot at each corner with 4 horizontal and 4 vertical fabric threads. Working from corners, use 8 fabric threads for each knot until all threads are knotted. Refer to photo to add buttons and ribbon as desired.

Design from Heartprint Greeting Cards, Inc.
Original artwork by Jan Jameson.
Needlework adaptation by Mike Vickery.

DIAGRAM

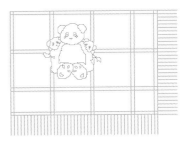

short end of afghan

Sweet treats can be "unbearably" tempting! While luring us into the kitchen to bake scrumptious goodies, this delightful design reminds us not to eat too many of them.

LIFE IS FULL OF

UPS AND POUNDS!

84w x 98h

X	DMC	¼X	B'ST	ANC.	COLOR	X	DMC	¼X	B'ST	ANC.	COLOR
•	blanc			2	white	☆	680			901	dk yellow
◉	309			42	pink	2	738			361	vy lt tan
✛	433			358	brown		798			131	vy dk blue
✖	434			310	lt brown	✕	799			136	dk blue
▯	435			1046	dk tan	□	800			144	lt blue
△	436			1045	tan	◖	809			130	blue
▭	437			362	lt tan	◼	816			1005	dk pink
S	562			210	green	▲	898			360	dk brown
V	563			208	lt green	◇	3326			36	lt pink
O	676			891	yellow	⦿	898				dk brown French Knot

The design was stitched on a 14" x 15" piece of Beige Aida (14 ct). Two strands of floss were used for Cross Stitch and 1 strand for Backstitch and French Knots. It was inserted in a cookbook holder (7" x 8" opening).

Design by Deb Meyer for Figi Graphics.

137

Spell out your love for Teddy with this colorful alphabet! We used the letters to personalize a shirt, but you can use your imagination to create a variety of projects.

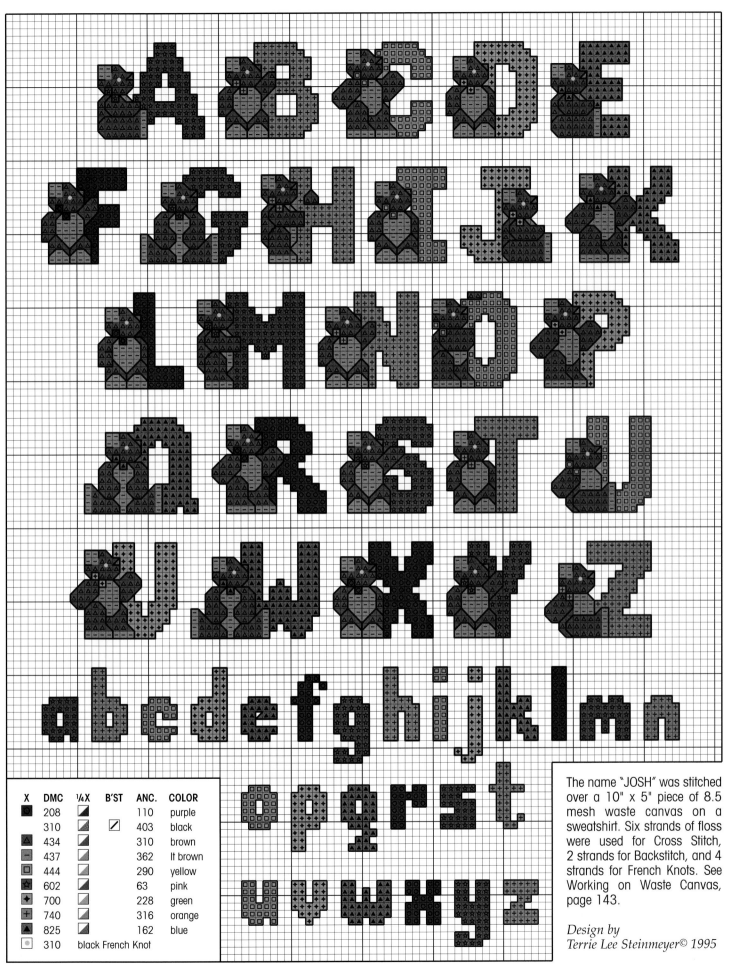

X	DMC	¼X	B'ST	ANC.	COLOR
◼	208	◪		110	purple
	310	◪	◿	403	black
◭	434	◪		310	brown
−	437	◪		362	lt brown
▢	444	◪		290	yellow
✽	602	◪		63	pink
◆	700	◪		228	green
✛	740	◪		316	orange
▲	825	◪		162	blue
◉	310	black French Knot			

The name "JOSH" was stitched over a 10" x 5" piece of 8.5 mesh waste canvas on a sweatshirt. Six strands of floss were used for Cross Stitch, 2 strands for Backstitch, and 4 strands for French Knots. See Working on Waste Canvas, page 143.

Design by
Terrie Lee Steinmeyer© 1995

With just a few loving stitches, a timeworn friend like Teddy can feel like new! This whimsical wall hanging is great for the sewing room.

...teddy bear repair...

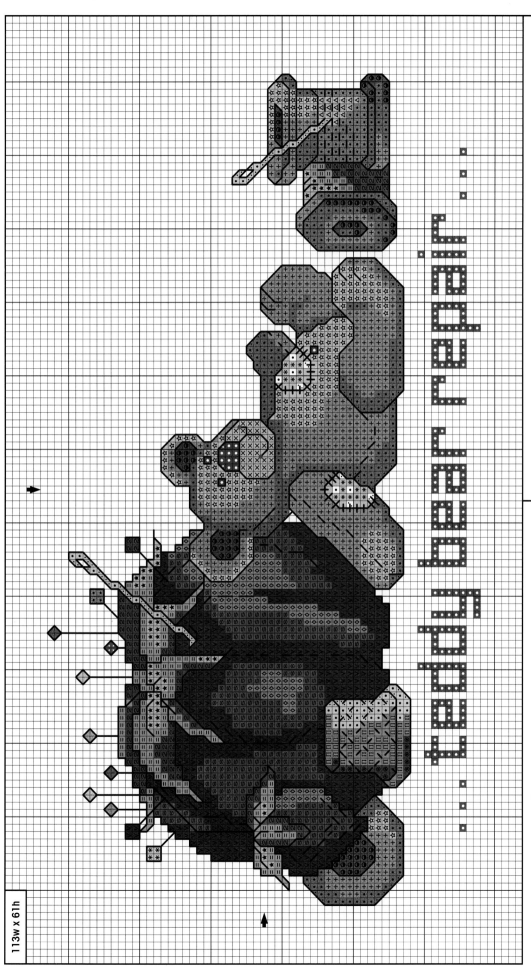

113w x 61h

teddy bear repair

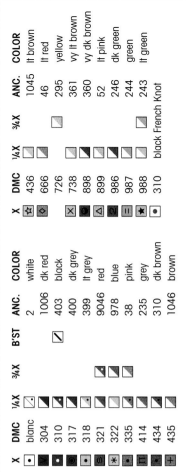

X	3/4X	1/4X	DMC	ANC.	COLOR
			436	1045	lt brown
			666	46	lt red
			726	295	yellow
			738	361	vy lt brown
			898	360	vy dk brown
			899	52	lt pink
			986	246	dk green
			987	244	green
			988	243	lt green
			310		black French Knot

X	3/4X	1/4X	B'ST	DMC	ANC.	COLOR
				blanc	2	white
				304	1006	dk red
				310	403	black
				317	400	dk grey
				318	399	lt grey
				321	9046	red
				322	978	blue
				335	38	pink
				414	235	grey
				434	310	dk brown
				435	1046	brown

The design was stitched on a 16" x 12" piece of Antique White Aida (14 ct). Three strands of floss were used for Cross Stitch and 1 strand for Backstitch and French Knots. It was made into a wall hanging. See "Teddy Bear Repair" Wall Hanging Finishing, page 144.

Design by Kathie Rueger.

GENERAL INSTRUCTIONS

WORKING WITH CHARTS

How to Read Charts: Each of the designs is shown in chart form. Each colored square on the chart represents one Cross Stitch or one Half Cross Stitch. Each colored triangle on the chart represents one One-Quarter Stitch or one Three-Quarter Stitch. Black or colored dots represent French Knots. Black or colored ovals represent Lazy Daisy Stitches. The straight lines on the chart indicate Backstitch. When a French Knot, Lazy Daisy Stitch, or Backstitch covers a square, the symbol is omitted or a reduced symbol is shown.

Each chart is accompanied by a color key. This key indicates the color of floss to use for each stitch on the chart. The headings on the color key are for Cross Stitch (**X**), DMC color number (**DMC**), One-Quarter Stitch (**¼X**), Three-Quarter Stitch (**¾X**), Half Cross Stitch (**½X**), Backstitch (**B'ST**), Anchor color number (**ANC**), and color name (**COLOR**). Color key columns should be read vertically and horizontally to determine type of stitch and floss color.

How to Determine Finished Size: The finished size of your design will depend on the thread count per inch of the fabric being used. To determine the finished size of the design on different fabrics, divide the number of squares (stitches) in the width of the charted design by the thread count of the fabric. For example, a charted design with a width of 80 squares worked on 14 count Aida will yield a design 5¾" wide. Repeat for the number of squares (stitches) in the height of the charted design. (**Note:** To work over two fabric threads, divide the number of squares by one-half the thread count.) Then add the amount of background you want plus a generous amount for finishing.

Where to Start: The horizontal and vertical centers of the charted design are shown by arrows. You may start at any point on the charted design, but be sure the design will be centered on the fabric. Locate the center of fabric by folding in half, top to bottom and again left to right. On the charted design, count the number of squares from the center of the chart to the determined starting point; then from the fabric's center, count out the same number of fabric threads.

STITCH DIAGRAMS

Counted Cross Stitch (X): For horizontal rows, work stitches in two journeys (**Fig. 1**). For vertical rows, complete each stitch as shown (**Fig. 2**). When working over two fabric threads, work Cross Stitch as shown in **Fig. 3**. When the chart shows a Backstitch crossing a colored square (**Fig. 4**), a Cross Stitch should be worked first; then the Backstitch (**Fig. 9 or 10**) should be worked on top of the Cross Stitch.

Fig. 1 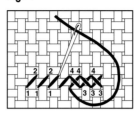 **Fig. 2**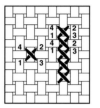

Fig. 3 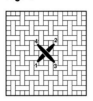 **Fig. 4**

Quarter Stitch (¼X and ¾X): Come up at 1 (**Fig. 5**); then split fabric thread to go down at 2. When stitches 1-4 are worked in the same color, the resulting stitch is called a Three-Quarter Stitch (**¾X**). When working over 2 fabric threads, work Quarter Stitches as shown in **Fig. 6**.

Fig. 5 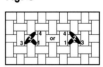 **Fig. 6**

Half Cross Stitch (½X): This stitch is one journey of the Cross Stitch and is worked from lower left to upper right as shown in **Fig. 7**. When working over two fabric threads, work Half Cross Stitch as shown in **Fig. 8**.

Fig. 7 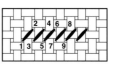 **Fig. 8**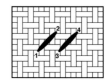

Backstitch (B'ST): For outline detail, Backstitch should be worked after the design has been completed (**Fig. 9**). When working over two fabric threads, work Backstitch as shown in **Fig. 10**.

Fig. 9 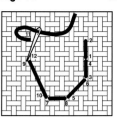 **Fig. 10**

French Knot: Bring needle up at 1. Wrap floss once around needle and insert needle at 2, holding floss with non-stitching fingers (**Fig. 11**). Tighten knot; then pull needle through fabric, holding floss until it must be released. For larger knot, use more strands; wrap only once.

Fig. 11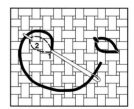

Lazy Daisy Stitch: Bring needle up at 1 and make a loop. Go down at 1 and come up at 2, keeping floss below point of needle (**Fig. 12**). Pull needle through and go down at 2 to anchor loop, completing stitch. (**Note:** To support stitches, it may be helpful to go down in edge of next fabric thread when anchoring loop.)

Fig. 12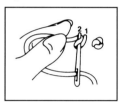